BETTER TENNIS

The author, right, instructs young tennis enthusiasts

Better Tennis

by

Harry Hopman

Coach to the Australian Davis Cup players

Kaye & Ward · London
in association with
Hicks, Smith & Sons
Australia and New Zealand

First published in the USA 1972
First published in Great Britain by
Kaye & Ward Ltd
1972

ISBN 0 7182 0486 7

All enquiries and requests relevant to this title
should be sent to the publisher, Kaye & Ward Ltd,
21 New Street, London EC2M 4NT, and not to the printer.

Printed in England by Fletcher & Son Ltd, Norwich.

Foreword

There are no hard and fast rules for learning to play tennis or for developing your game, and there is no one style which could be laid down as the 'correct' way to play.

To stress this very important aspect of tennis I refer to the top Australian Davis Cup players of the past twenty years, beginning with the successful 1950 team of John Bromwich, Frank Sedgman and Ken McGregor. Other big names come up in the following order: Merv Rose, Lew Hoad, Ken Rosewall, Rex Hartwig, Mal Anderson, Ashley Cooper, Neale Fraser, Rod Laver, Roy Emerson, John Newcombe, Fred Stolle and Tony Roche.

I was associated with them as captain of their teams in all their Davis Cup successes and other triumphs, coaching and advising them in many ways on and off the court. I got to know them and their games better than they knew themselves or how they played.

They all played differently in the way they stroked the ball, as evidenced by Laver's heavily topped backhand passing shot and Rosewall's firm and strong slice. They had similar basic fitness training, but their day-to-day training differed with some of them in the amount of work they liked to do and needed to reach and maintain top form; and although most were basically net-rushers, their tactics differed in many ways to accommodate their individual styles and their evaluations of various opponents.

None of these champions played the same game. Bromwich used two hands for forehand drives and volleys and was righthanded for service and smashing. He was lefthanded for any stroke on the left side. He preferred to play mainly from the back of the court, whereas most of the others were net-rushers. He hit his forehand most of the time with the same kind of slight underspin Rosewall uses on his backhand. He relied on the accuracy and consistency of his ground strokes to bring mistakes from his opponents, whereas Sedgman and Emerson sought to force errors with aggressive volleying and smashing in much the same way as Fraser tore apart many an opposition game with the power, break and slice of his big lefthanded deliveries; and Hoad paves the way for his all-court power with the speed of his serving. Rosewall, Anderson, Cooper, Stolle and

Newcombe are known best for their smooth ground strokes, but their games don't look like the top-spinning game of Laver as he just as smoothly hits his way through many of the major tournaments. You must conclude that most, if not all, champions are different. Your own style could be one of the most important decisions you will make in tennis. You should take great care in deciding on which champion you should model your strokes and your natural approach to the game; you should give much thought to deciding whether to change any stroke which may feel natural; and you should be wary of any coach who tells you there is only one way to make certain strokes or only one way to play certain shots. Most of the champions I have mentioned here had had no coaching when they began to play, and they developed their different styles to suit their physical makeup, temperament and personality.

Aspects of the game, other than strokemaking, in which all the champions I have mentioned were given much assistance, are training, tactics, temperament (which, of course, embraces behaviour on and off the court), courtcraft, pride of performance and many other things which are necessary for successful competitive tennis under pressure.

There is much to learn. Some of it may be a little dry and unexciting, but you can get your excitement when you next step on court and try some of the 'How to Improve' hints I will give. When you do play, try to remember that tennis is like every other sport, in that if you wish to improve your game you must work at it, give it concentration and remember that essentially it is a sport and good exercise.

Contents

Photographs by Robert Crane of the Garcia-Cragin Corporation, except where otherwise indicated. Photographs 21, 38–43 by courtesy of Le-Roye Productions Ltd. Photographs 51, 53–55 by courtesy of D.D. and E. Peter Schroeder.

Introduction

I would like you to play better tennis.

The essential qualities of a tennis champion are concentration, discipline and determination because they are necessary for the many hours of hard work needed to acquire the technical skill, physical abilities and mental approach to reach championship class, and for the continued improvement from that stage if your goal is set for the very top.

I have seen these qualities blossom in so many of the young people I have helped on their way to stardom that I am convinced that striving for improvement on the practice court and in the tougher match play of tournaments is character-building.

Unlike many school authorities, I believe there is more character-building to be found in tennis than in so-called team games, such as cricket in Britain and Australia and the many types of football now played almost the world over. If the sharing of triumph and disaster—and the necessary teamwork to achieve one and overcome the other—are required, I can recommend the understanding and teamwork of the successful doubles combination.

I find much satisfaction in following the fortunes of the former Davis Cup players, especially those who continue to travel the tournaments, because I spent many more months of each year with some of them when they were developing into champions than they spent with their families. All of them were world travellers in their 'teens and, because they were healthy youths, could have been badly spoiled in many ways. Instead, they made friends for themselves and Australia around the world and profited by meeting fine people associated with the game, as well as getting greater pleasure than most by playing winning tennis, becoming famous and making their fortunes. One asset they all possessed before they set their sights for the top was a great love for the game. Fortunately you also will possess this love if you trouble to read this book. You will find it a love which will grow as you learn more about it, and as tennis is a game which can be played from a very early age until late in life, it has been truly said for many that tennis has been their love of a lifetime.

Tennis terms

Here is a list of tennis terms in case you have difficulty in understanding some of those used in this book or those to be heard around your tennis club:

Point The smallest unit of score in tennis. It takes four winning points to make a game unless both sides have each won three of the first six points, when the score is deuce (sometimes referred to as forty-all). From that stage one side must gain the next two points to win the game—if the score is back to deuce, then another effort is made to put one side ahead by two points.

Game Begins from love-all and then could go (if each side wins alternate points) to 15-0, 15-15, 30-15, 30-30, 40-30, deuce. The next point is advantage server or receiver. The next point takes it to game or back to deuce.

Set Can go to the side first reaching six games. This is a short set. What is generally known as a long set is that from five-all: either side must reach two games ahead of the other—say 7-5 or 10-8—to win the set.

Recently what is known as the *tie-breaker* set has been introduced. It can be varied depending on what a tournament committee wishes. If a score reaches, let us say, six-all, then the next five or seven or nine—or, if you wish an even number, six or eight or twelve—are played with each taking two successive services. If an odd number of points is to be used, one side gets an advantage of an additional service point. If an even number is used and each side wins the same number of points, then it is tried again. Naturally, the side to win the number to gain a winning advantage—say five points in a nine-point tie-breaker—wins the set.

Set point A point which would give one side the set. It could come, for instance, at 5-4 and 40-30.

Match Can be determined as any length. In championship play it is usually the best two out of three sets for women and junior players and the best three out of five sets for men. In club play the first to reach x number of games—say eight or ten—can be a match.

Ace An untouchable service. It is often confused with a big service that the receiver touches but fails to return.

Service The first stroke of each point; it can be hit overhead, sidearm or underarm.

Service fault A service where you throw up the ball, swing at it and miss, or when the service ball you do hit fails to land in the correct service court.

Double fault The failure of the server to put either of the two services allowed for each point into the correct court.

Foot fault This occurs when the server puts a foot on the baseline or any part of the court inside the line while he is going through the action of service and before he has struck the ball.

Let Another service for the service played when the ball touches the net and falls into the correct service court. A let is also called when interference of some kind is judged by the central umpire to have had some effect on the play, not necessarily only on service.

Ground strokes Hitting the ball after it has bounced. The ball must be played before it hits the ground a second time.

Forehand A ground stroke on the right side of a righthander. (Vice versa for a lefthander.)

Backhand A ground stroke on the left side of a righthander. (Vice versa for a lefthander.)

Half volley This occurs when the ball is hit as it hits the ground or very early on the rise.

Volley Hitting the ball on the full (while it is in the air) and usually from about head height to the ground.

Smash Hitting the ball on the full and usually taken above head height. Sometimes a high lob is allowed to bounce and then, if the ball rises high enough on the bound, it is smashed.

Lob To send the ball over the head and racket of the player at the net. It is used defensively when retrieving shots and especially when an opponent has smashed well. It is often hit high mainly to allow time to regain good court position. It is used also in attack to remind an opponent not to get too close to the net for volleys, or when you know an opponent has a poor overhead (smash). Then the lob is usually lower and aimed only just over the out-stretched racket of the opposition.

Lob volley A touch shot infrequently used because there is little margin for error. When opponents are in close a volley is lobbed over their heads.

Drop volley A touch shot which drops a volley just over the net, sometimes also at an angle. Usually played, of course, when the opposition is near the baseline—far from the net.

Drop shot This should be a deceptive shot with an opponent in the backcourt or behind the baseline. It is played with underspin so that the ball, when it does land just over the net, will stop short on the bounce.

Chop As its name indicates, it is played with an action similar to chopping wood with the racket passing abruptly across the flight of the ball to impart heavy underspin.

Slice The racket passes under the ball with the wrist about a quarter of a turn clockwise to impart slice to the ball.

Baseline game A player stays mainly within a few feet of the baseline. It is often termed a backcourt game.

Net game As implied, the player gets to the forecourt (near the net) at every opportunity—even taking risks to get there—so as to use volleys and overhead strokes.

Passing shot A drive which passes an opponent at the net.

Down-the-line A shot played parallel to, and close to, the sideline.

Crosscourt A shot played diagonally across court from one corner to the opposite corner.

Approach shot A shot hit to any part of the opponent's court and which the player believes will be sufficiently effective to bring a reply with which he can deal at, or close to, the net.

Change of length Exactly what it says, and often used to try to force an opponent into error; to break up the opponent's rhythm. It is usually thought of as one deep shot followed by a short shot or a medium-court shot.

Change of pace or **Change of speed** Often used because some opponents can handle speed but don't do so well off slow shots. This is especially so of slow, deep shots with a high bound to the backhand side of most players.

No-man's-land Between a yard inside the baseline and the service line and usually a bad spot for any but a good player who can move sideways fast and volley or half-volley from that depth of court.

Grips There are three widely known grips, Eastern, Continental and Western, but the first two dominate play today.

Singles For two players; doubles is for four—two each end.

Spin Spin the ball by hitting over it (top spin), under it (for the chop [sometimes called a chip shot, a misnomer because the chip is a very mild and short version of the chop] and underspin), and hitting side-on and downward for the slice.

11

Twist Another form of spin put on service. Slice is often put on service also, used mainly to try to take an opponent out of court.

Footwork One of the most important essentials of good play. Footwork is different for many strokes, and good footwork usually leads to good *timing* which leads to *pace of a stroke* (as opposed to speed).

Return-of-service Putting the service back into play. This is a particular phase of the game where good fast footwork is often an essential because of the speed and control of many services and the very little time one has to prepare to play the service.

Rally An exchange of shots to win a point.

Forced error An error made off an opposition shot which is so good that it forces a mistake.

Placement A winning shot, other than a service ace, which the opposition cannot touch.

Pressure Used in the tennis sense of making things difficult for an opponent, such as a strong service to good position on an opponent's weakness followed by a rush to good position toward the net at match point against the opponent.

Tactics and strategy They are closely related in that both are involved in using one's talents to greatest effect against the opposition weaknesses.

The all-court player One who can play well from any part of the court and whose strokes and shots produce good results.

The REFEREE of a tournament, the UMPIRE and LINESMEN Officials who are doing their best, usually in an honorary capacity, and should be treated with great respect.

Ranking Placing in an order of ability on performance.

Seeding A tournament seeding is usually based on performance, with emphasis on recent play, the annual ranking and the outcome of the same tournament a year earlier. For instance, a titleholder is usually given some preference when defending the title.

Grand slam of tennis The four championships—in their order of play each year: Australia, France, England (Wimbledon) and the United States. Don Budge won it once, in 1938, and Rod Laver, twice, in 1962 and 1969.

Senior player One over forty-five years. There are various age-groups over that mark.

The highest body in tennis is the International Lawn Tennis Federation, usually referred to as the I.L.T.F., comprising sixty-six countries with voting rights and twenty-seven associate member countries.

The highest association in the U.K. is the Lawn Tennis Association (L.T.A.).

The highest association in American tennis is the United States Lawn Tennis Association, usually known as the U.S.L.T.A.

The major worldwide trophy of the game is the Davis Cup for men's national team play; next comes the Federation Cup for women's national team play.

Sportsmanship

Sportsmanship is something that you cannot steal or buy
Because it is a product of how hard you really try.
It is the emblem of the soul as you are most sincere
In striving to be worthy of each handshake and each cheer.
It is the spirit of the heart you put into a game
To play it hard without regard to any claim to fame.
And more importantly the strength to take it standing up
When you believe you should have won a medal or a cup.
Sportsmanship is striving hard and taking things in stride
As you perform your best so God is always on your side.

Some sporting habits and goals have changed since the above was written, but it reflects a standard of behaviour that applies today.

Tennis has had and will always have some players unable to discipline themselves under pressure, and so an ugly side of their nature emerges. But it is no coincidence, in view of the many fine attributes necessary to attain major ambitions, that it is difficult to recall a Wimbledon or United States champion who was not also a fine sportsman.

If I take alone the Australian champions of the past twenty years, with all of whom I was closely associated, who won either the Wimbledon or the United States title, and some of them both, it is also no coincidence that Frank Sedgman (won both), Lew Hoad, Ken Rosewall, Mal Anderson, Ashley Cooper (both), Neale Fraser (both), Rod Laver (both), Roy Emerson (both), Fred Stolle and John Newcombe (both) were not tantrum-throwers or racket-flingers, did not use bad language on the courts or engage in running verbal battles with linesmen, umpires or galleries as they won their way to the playing heights some of them continue to maintain.

It was noticeable with them, however, that when things were going badly they strived harder to maintain concentration. They accepted the bad breaks along with the opposition's fine bursts of play as inevitable (after all, in the major championships there are usually a number of others who think they can win) and continued to struggle, to fight with all their determination. When the dust of battle had lifted, they were always ready to accept victory modestly and defeat gracefully.

You don't have to wear a large smile to show you don't mind being defeated. Most likely you do mind a lot, and if you did not play your best, you are no doubt disappointed. But it costs nothing to mask your disappointment with a smile. The main guard you should have up in defeat is against saying something you could regret. It is very easy to fall into a habit of speaking your mind as you come off court from a tough match when things have not gone your way and you believe justice has not been done. Then, silence is a virtue. A hasty word, especially among people who don't understand the very heavy pressures of match play, can brand you as a poor sportsman.

You must realize that you are going to have some bad days among, you hope, many good ones. Think of those bad days as times when your opponent is causing the trouble by having good days. Keep your excuses to yourself and use them to reason how you lost. *Give your opponent credit for success*. If it is your turn to show best form next time, I am sure you will want to hear his 'Well done!'

Sportsmanship is shown in many ways other than by a pleasant court demeanour and the ability to accept success and defeat with grace. Always it involves good manners: Don't keep your opponent waiting for the start of a match or at the end of the usual interval.

If you don't have ballboys or an umpire, it is important that you call shots quickly and distinctly enough for your opponent to hear, even if at the time you have your back to him. You should give him the benefit of any doubt, but at the same time don't call against yourself if you did not see the ball well enough to make a decision. Give notice immediately if you believe you have erred with a double-hit, you have touched the net with your racket or clothing, that the ball touched your clothing or your body, or that you have failed to 'make' the ball which appears a possible double-bounce. When returning balls to the server's end between points, try to hit them to the opponent and attract his attention so there is no undue delay or ball-chasing.

Don't stall. I doubt if there is a violation worse than intentional stalling in any of its many forms, such as towelling between change-ends games (no referee should tolerate more than sixty seconds), moving around the court for any purpose at very slow speed, delay at the end of a set which might end on even games and where a rest should not be taken, making a 'ceremony' of returning a ball strayed from an adjacent court or clearing the court of balls between services, and last but certainly not least of these few nasty examples, is the stall in excess of the allowable ten-minute interval.

Next time you have an opportunity to watch any of the champions I mentioned earlier, or such players as the members of the American Davis Cup winning team of 1970, Arthur Ashe, Stan Smith, Cliff Richey and Bob Lutz, pay special attention to their court demeanour. One reason they have been or are champions is that they have learned from experience that no one can afford to give away points and that one of the most stupid ways of giving points away is to become upset and lose concentration.

Sportsmanship and courtesy go hand in hand throughout a tennis tournament. There are many little things one can do that keep the game enjoyable for all—the organizers and other officials as well as the players. You can think of many yourself, and you should take the trouble to do so; but I remind you of a few, such as advising the tournament committee of your arrival, later thanking the umpire and, without fail, shaking hands with your opponent. If you are being accommodated by a member of the club, small courtesies to your hosts are always happily received. If you play doubles there are many things to be done to make the partnership pleasant, but the most important is to understand that, like yourself, your partner is going to have some poor matches of play, some poor days, and when those bad moments occur a warm word is wonderfully encouraging.

The people who can assist young players in their ambitions to be great are usually watching and they warm to those who are courteous, who give their best in defeat and show qualities of good sportsmanship.

Scoring

Points in tennis are called love, 15, 30, 40, deuce, advantage.

THE GAME

0, or nothing, is called love. First point won by a player is called 15. Second point won by a player is called 30. Third point won by a player is called 40. Fourth point won by a player gives him game. Except that: If each player has won three points (40-all) the score is deuce. Then the next point won by a player gives him advantage, but if he then loses the next point, the score is again deuce.

From a score of 40-all or deuce a player must win two points in succession to win a game.

The server's score is always called first. For instance:

Server	Receiver	Score
1 point	0 points	15-love
2 points	0 points	30-love
3 points	0 points	40-love
4 points	0 points	game to the server
1 point	1 point	15-all
2 points	3 points	30-40
4 points	5 points	receiver's advantage
4 points	6 points	receiver's game

THE SET

The first player to win six games wins a set, provided he is at least two games ahead of his opponent (6-2, 6-3, 7-5, 8-6, etc.).

In men's play matches generally consist of either two out of three sets or three out of five sets. In women's play it is generally two out of three sets.

SUDDEN DEATH SCORING

In the event of a set's score being tied at 5 games all (a sudden death set can be fixed at 6-all or any figure to suit the organizers unless play is under the rules of some governing body which says otherwise), he who would normally serve the eleventh game of a 9-point sudden death tie-breaker shall serve points 1, 2, 5, 6. Ends of the court shall be changed after the first four points—after each player has served two points in succession. If the score is 4 points all, the ends shall not be changed again, and the receiver of the first two points of the tie-breaker shall serve the ninth point, while the receiver has the right to say whether the service must be in the first or the second court.

At the end of the tie-break game the receiver of the first two points of the tie-breaker (regardless of how many points the tie-breaker took) shall commence serving in the second set. In the event of the score being again tied in the second set at 5-all (or whatever figure-all is set), the server whose turn it is to serve in that set shall serve points 1, 2, 5, 6 of the tie-break game, etc.

If the sets are tied 1-all in a three-set match or 2-all in a five-set match, the players shall spin again for choice of service or side in the final set. Umpires should note that if this results in a change of serving sequence, the next ball change, if any, should be deferred one game to preserve the alternation of the right to serve first with new balls.

In doubles one player on Team A serves points 1 and 2, and his partner 5 and 6. On Team B one player serves points 3 and 4, and his partner 7, 8 and 9. Each player shall serve from the same end of the court in the tie-break game that he has served from during that particular set.

The tie-break sequence shall count as one game for ball-change reckoning.

RULES OF VASS 'SINGLE POINT'   (VASS stands for Van Alen Simplified Scoring System)

It is scored as in table tennis: 1, 2, 3, 4, 5, etc.

The service changes from one player (or one pair) to another every five points (5, 10, 15, etc.). The player or team receiving on the fifth point of each service sequence may choose to receive in the right or left court. The first service in each sequence of five must, however, be served into the right court.

Ends of court are changed on the 'odd five' points (5, 15, 25). Sets are usually 31 points, but there is nothing to prevent a set of 21 points.

The winner of the set must lead by at least two points (31-29). At 30 points all, sudden death (tie-breaker) decides set winner.

Service changes sides at the end of each set.

Grips

If you have a grip and stroke that are troubling you, and you lack confidence to 'go for' the placement you wish to make, or fail to control the flight of the ball, don't necessarily believe that you must stick with them until you 'conquer' them. On the contrary, ask someone competent to advise if the grip or the stroke you are making with it is reasonably sound. Ask if you should make a change. I can assure you it is never too late to make changes in your game. Don't lose sight of the fact that tennis is a game for a lifetime. It is better to make when young a change of something that would be a handicap for life. During my already long tennis experience of fifty-two years, I have often seen good players go through a career with one handicap that prevented them from playing better and which they could have avoided fairly easily—with practice—at some early stage of their tennis game.

I have advised some of the finest Australian champions over the past twenty years to alter a stroke, and although the change set them back temporarily, they went on to heights greater than I believe they would have otherwise attained.

Your choice of grip could be one of the most important decisions of your tennis career. Regardless of the physical and mental attributes you bring to the game, the grip you use will have the most bearing on the type of game you play. For instance, you could begin with a grip which might prevent your ever having a reliable attacking service and overhead, and without them you would probably elect to become a baseliner or back-of-the-court player, seldom going to the net.

There are two common grips, the *Eastern* and the *Continental,* and one in occasional use, the *Western.* I mention the Western grip but don't advocate it. Forty to seventy years ago, when there were many asphalt-type courts and tennis balls bounced higher, the Western grip was popular, and a little (9 stone 4 pounds) Californian, W. M. (Bill) Johnston, using this grip to generate great power, was probably the best player in the world in 1919. Now I believe there are too many problems with short- and low-bounding balls on many slow types of courts for a player with the Western grip to become the world's Number One. I suggest you settle for the Eastern or the Continental and the many slight variations between those two grips.

As you read this, please remember that here I am advocating two grips and at the same time telling you there are many different strokes in the game and several different varieties of most of these strokes, such as flat, kick and break, as well as spin and/or slice in service. With this in mind the grip you choose should feel comfortable enough to be adaptable because, as you improve in the game, there will be many occasions when slight variations in your strokes must be made almost without thought.

Even when you are beginning, knowing which is the right grip for the stroke you wish to make—and knowing it quickly—makes life easier because it gets your racket into position quickly, and that makes for accuracy.

If you are not a beginner, and the grip and strokes you have are natural and quite different from those I advocate, then continue to use them confidently. But make sure they are sound and not interfering with all-round development and not taking too much out of you physically.

If you are an advanced club player, don't be afraid to change a grip which is retarding progress. It is never too late to learn new strokes, and they don't necessarily take long to learn if you already know the fundamentals of stroking the ball. It may upset your game while a change is in progress but, set against a lifetime of play, a short upheaval should not deter the experiment of a change.

Every Wimbledon, United States, French and Australian winner I have watched has had some difference in style, but almost all of them enjoyed a completeness of strokemaking which left them without a weakness. Therefore, if you are ambitious, don't allow one stroke to upset or restrict the rest of your game. Scrap it and learn another.

I prefer the Eastern grip to the Continental. It has a greater margin for safety in the all-round game of attack and defence because it has a little natural top-spin which, with very slight change in stroke production, can be turned into either heavier top-spin or into a flat drive with less risk than the Continental.

Of several ways to 'find' the Eastern forehand grip I believe the simplest is as in pictures 1, 2, 3, and 4. Hold your racket edge-on and at the throat. Place your hand flat on the strings and then slide your open palm down the racket to the end of the handle or grip. Try it that way and then compare what you have with the pictures. It is also known as the 'shake hands' grip, so try it again holding the racket the same way and simply

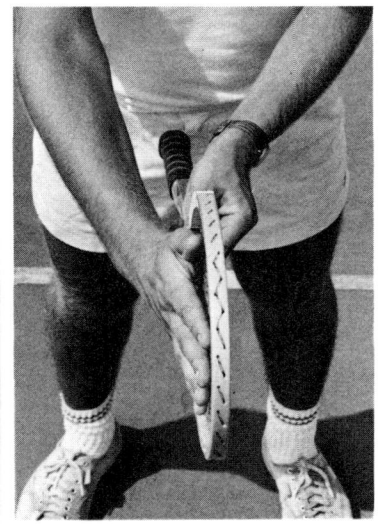

1, 2, 3 Eastern forehand grip   **2**   **3**

shaking hands with the grip. Hold the racket out in front of you with the line of the arm and racket straight or at a very slight angle.

To change to the Eastern backhand, turn your hand (your grip) between one-eighth to a quarter-circle counterclockwise (if you are righthanded, and the reverse, of course, if lefthanded) to put your hand more on top of the handle of the racket. You can have your thumb around the handle or, if you feel you get greater strength from putting the thumb down or up the handle, then by all means try it. Certainly try the thumb up or down for low balls near the ground. Because of the difficulty I have noticed some up (or down)-the-handle thumb players experience with low-bounding strokes, I advocate the thumb around the grip. The arm and racket again should form a straight, or nearly straight, line.

Some coaches advocate a stiff and locked wrist with the racket upwards at approximately a 45-degree angle, but no champion uses this 'angled and locked wrist' action, though some do admit to having learned that way and having changed before they reached championship status because of its limitations in stroke production.

Some prominent players have used the Eastern forehand grip for both backhand and forehand, but I suggest you try to change. Most 'How to Play' books written more than thirty years ago spoke of the service and volleying grip, when using the Eastern grip, to be about halfway between the forehand and backhand grips. In the past thirty years, however, so

21

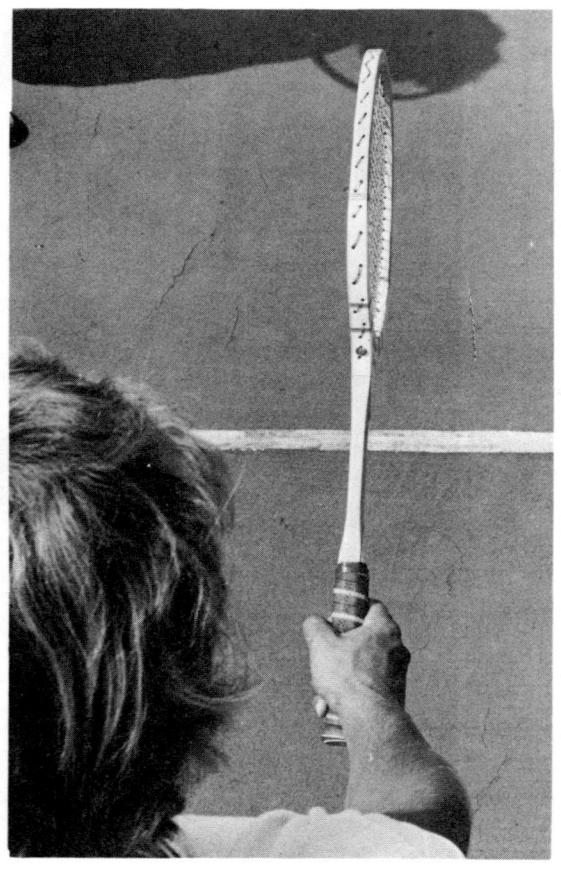

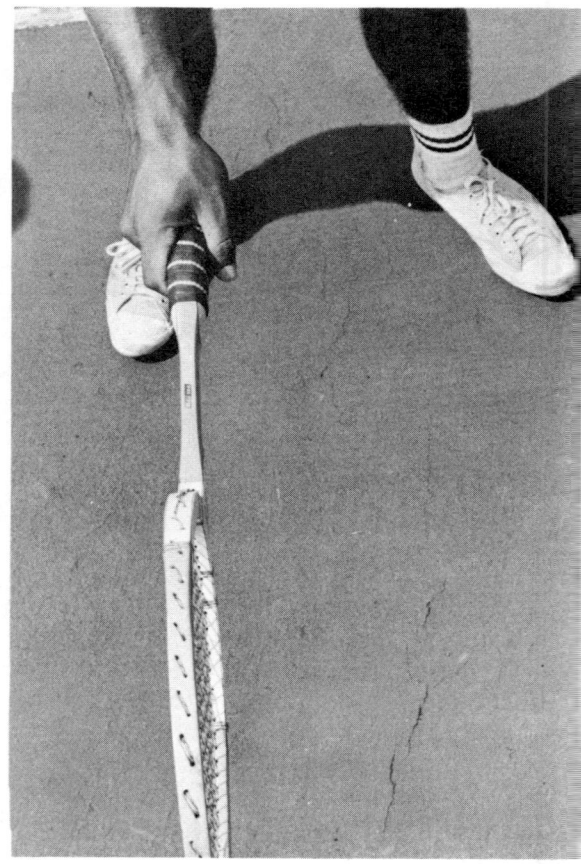

4 This is the Eastern forehand grip as you should see it when holding the racket in the correct manner

5 Continental grip

many players of world standard have used the Eastern forehand grip also for the volley—by using the forearm for power and turning the wrist for placement—that I believe the volleying grip must be left to individual choice. It is the same with service: Many champions have shown exceptional services with grips all the way between those two Eastern grips— forehand and backhand.

The Continental grip (see picture 5) is about halfway between the Eastern forehand and backhand. It does not appear to be a major change as you hold a racket and swing, but when seeking control on court the Continental forehand grip requires a strong wrist for consistency and for

22

6

6, 7 Western forehand grip

7

accurate timing because any necessary top-spin control comes from the wrist movement. There is no natural top-spin on it, and the spin imparted by wrist movement increases the margin for error. On the credit side is the fact that the grip can be used for all strokes and is, to most, the easiest one for hitting a very low ball with a flat drive. The Continental was in greater favour in the 1930s than now because England's great Fred Perry used it effectively, especially when playing the ball on the run, winning three Wimbledon singles titles in a row (1934–5–6) and performing brilliantly in Davis Cup play.

A simple way to 'find' the Western grip is to lay your racket on the ground and pick it up (see pictures 6 and 7). You should be gripping the handle about a quarter-turn further around the handle clockwise than for the Eastern forehand. If you have it correctly the grip should feel awkward.

23

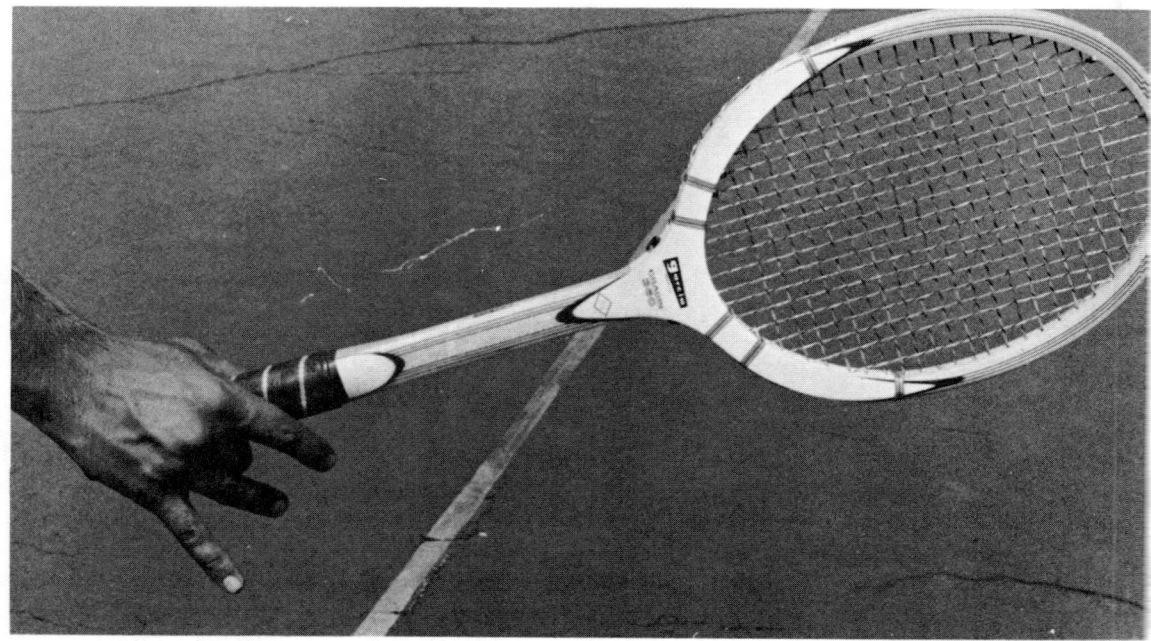

8 Comfort is the main concern when you are deciding whether to wrap your fingers close together around the racket grip or to spread them slightly, as most players do. You can see that the thumb and middle finger are most used for grip

The most interesting thing about the Western grip is that all strokes are hit with the same face of the racket and not the opposite face, as used for backhand and forehand with the Eastern and Continental grips. The Western forehand automatically produces top-spin and if the same full swing is used on the backhand side it again produces top-spin. On both sides the top-spin is usually 'heavy' or exaggerated, with the ball dropping sharply. However, of the few who now use the Western grip, some often hit top-spin on the forehand and use a heavy block-slice on the backhand side. The Western grip is very limited in both strokemaking and finesse, and it is many years since a player using this grip has won Top Ten world ranking.

Ground strokes

For some reason I can never understand, most less-skilled players take a 'ready' position a yard or more behind the baseline to receive service in match play or when practising. *This is entirely wrong.* More ground strokes are played at this level of ability around the middle of the court than within a yard or two of the baseline. Therefore, in practice as well as in match play, the 'ready' position should be at the baseline, with the player ready to skip back a yard or so, if necessary, to move well toward the short balls.

Don't practise by taking all the short balls on the second bounce. It is much better practice for you to get up to all the short balls on the first bounce, and if you cannot move back in time to drive a few of the balls which would land near the baseline, then volley them—hit them on the full.

And . . . keep your eye on the ball.

There are many different ways of stroking forehands and backhands with the varying grips used, but all these strokes are heavily dependent on good footwork for consistency and accuracy (see pictures 9–12).

Sometimes the ball will go where you want it despite poor footwork. An occasional champion can 'get away' with poor footwork because his balance and 'racket work' are better than average. Usually, however, the champion is as much concerned with his footwork as the young and ambitious player.

I want to stress that, before you try to do what I suggest should be done for all strokes of the game, you repeat over and over again, 'I must watch the ball at all times—and watch it right onto my racket.' It is important to players at all levels of the game, and I have said it to Australia's Davis Cup champions over the past twenty years as often as to novices.

One further piece of advice before you begin hitting your next forehand: When you are waiting service—standing at the ready, so to speak—don't stand with your weight on your toes. I have heard many advise 'be on your toes' to receive service. This is wrong in that it is not the easiest position from which to move fast, and in addition it puts a strain on the leg muscles.

Stand as relaxed and well balanced as possible (see picture 13). If you

9–12 Everything about this forehand action shot looks excellent. Seventeen-year-old Bill Durham was a student at my 1970 Summer Coaching School at Amherst College, USA, at the time this photograph was taken. He has approached the ball with good judgment, his weight on his back foot, racket well back before he reached the ball and his eyes on the ball. His knees are bent, with good body balance; he is about to transfer his weight forward into the stroke. (See picture 9)

9

In picture 10, with his left foot forward to take the body weight as it goes through and knees bending a little lower, he still has his eyes on the ball as his racket is about to make contact.

10

In picture 11 his eyes are still following the ball immediately after striking it and his weight a little further through onto the front (left) foot.

11

In picture 12 he follows the flight of his shot and finishes the stroke with his racket high—showing that he had some slight overspin on the ball. His weight has followed through as he finishes the stroke with good balance and is prepared to begin recovery to the ready.

12

feel that you can move more quickly when slightly crouched, then take that stance. You should have a firm grip on your racket, but don't hold it so tightly as to give the impression you wish to break it.

Watch the ball closely and move your feet well. In those two fundamentals of tennis lies the transference of weight into the ball you hit with good timing to give the pace (better known as speed) to your shots.

The ideal in footwork for stroke production would be to have your feet in position so that every stroke in the game except service could be hit with your body at right-angles (side on) to the net. Unfortunately there is not time to take up such a position for many of the shots much of the time, the

13 Young Australian Bill Durham is relaxed and ready to receive service.

13

volleys and half-volleys especially. However, for groundstrokes the sideways-to-the-net position is a must.

You wait for service usually facing the server and with feet spread a little to give good balance. As soon as you see the direction of the service you must make every effort to turn sideways so that, if the ball is coming within easy reach on your forehand side, your left foot is closer to the net and your weight slightly back on your right foot. Even if the ball is going wide to your forehand and you must stretch both legs and arms, the left foot should be foreward and closer to the ball and your body will have turned sideways to the net and parallel to the sideline. Try that as you read, and without a racket in your hand, if you wish. You will find that as you stretch wide to a ball your body will still be sideways to the net because your neck and head turn—rather than your shoulders—as you watch the flight of the ball.

Now try the backhand action, which is the reverse. A righthander in turning to hit a backhand shot will have his right foot closer to the net, and it will be in front and stretched wide when reaching for a wide ball. In both cases every effort should be made to reach the ball so that your weight will be moving into the stroke (toward the net) as you make the shot.

In both these strokes, and for almost all strokes in the game, there must be a transference of weight from the back to the front foot. You can see the transference of weight, as well as the footwork I have talked about, in the strip pictures shown here (14–20); how well they show, too, that the eyes have been kept on the ball. Don't expect to meet the ball as well as Adi Kourim and Bill Durham have done in their photographs. It takes experience to acquire that judgment and often a little skip-step at the right time to meet the ball exactly. Work out your own salvation in this; you may have the judgment to arrive at the ball just right—without crowding (getting too close to) your stroke or having to reach too far—and therefore require no 'additives'.

If you think you have the right idea so far I want you to look again at those strip photographs of Durham and Kourim. Note how they have taken their rackets back early, preparing for the stroke before they reach the ball, and try to do it.

The beginner in tennis usually arrives at the ball before starting to play a stroke. The champion begins his stroke well before reaching the ball and hits it as he reaches it. If the champion needs to prepare his stroke that carefully, you can imagine how difficult it is, in the rush, for the beginner to make a stroke upon arriving at the ball.

14

15

You must begin your swing—your stroke—on the way to the ball.
   Having struck the ball you must follow through with your racket, and
your weight must also 'go into the stroke'. Look again at those strips to
see how it is done. The completion of your stroke is dependent on the
type of stroke used—flat, spin, slice or cut (chop)—and the power put
into it.
   Most importantly: Don't lock your wrist for ground strokes. This
method is sometimes taught, but I can recall only two great champions,
René Lacoste and Jean Borotra (on the backhand)—both Frenchmen at
their greatest in the 1920s—to have used it successfully, and their origi-
nality in strokemaking was comparable to that of John Bromwich's two-
handed forehand.

30

14–20 Eyes on the ball, racket going back to prepare to move into the stroke and the left leg about to move forward. Bill Durham will be able to put his weight into the shot and at the same time maintain good balance to be able to recover quickly if the ball comes back. Note that Bill's eyes are on the ball all the time; in the third picture (16) see how well he retains his balance. The bounce of the ball Adi Kourim is going to hit (picture 17) will be much lower than that for Bill's forehand drive, judging by the bent knees as Adi moves to the ball. But the eyes are on the ball, the right foot (left for forehand) moves into position so that he can put weight into the shot and retain good balance on the high follow-through.

16

CONTROL OF THE BALL

The ball will always go where your racket determines and not always where you wish it to go. It may seem silly to say it, but few tennis players fully realize that fact. Most know where they want to hit the ball but fail to put the right control on the ball to take it there.

Grand Slam winner of 1969, Rod Laver, uses mainly top-spin for his control. The United States Open winner of 1970, Ken Rosewall, uses a firm slight slice for the great control he displays on his backhand. Margaret Court, the Grand Slam winner among women for 1970, uses slice for the consistency of her backhand, and the last of the really great women players, 'Li'l Mo' Connolly, hit winners on forehand and backhand with

17   18

pace from good timing and strokes almost flàt.

For spin and slice, swerve and curve, and kick and speed on service, I doubt there has been better for many years than the 1959 and 1960 United States singles winner, lefthander Neale Fraser of Australia. Fraser brought the spins and swerves of the cricket ball to tennis and improved on them to have the most feared service in the game for several years.

First you must know that the flat-hit tennis ball is the fastest in the game, and that spin and its relatives slow up the speed of the ball. You might ask, 'So why use spin?' The reason is that spin brings control and, in its varying forms and under certain conditions and against some opponents, can be a great asset in forcing opposition errors.

Most forehand drives carry some spin over the ball, i.e. top-spin, and most backhand drives carry some underslice or underspin. Even the flat

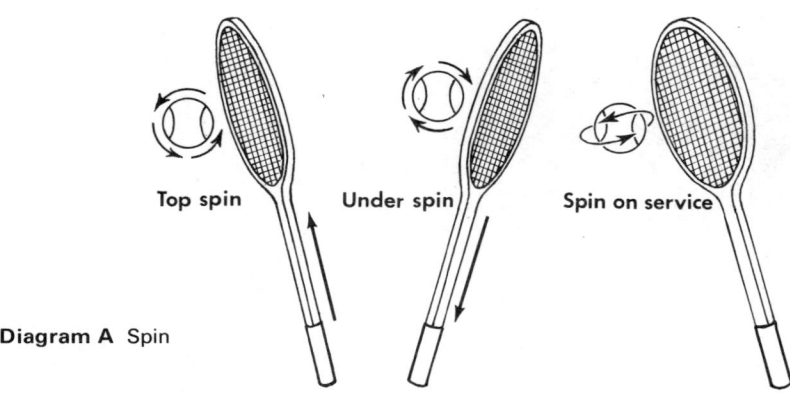

Top spin   Under spin   Spin on service

Diagram A Spin

drive of many players has a little natural spin on it from the action of the wrist or racket or both. The Eastern forehand, for instance, carries a little top-spin, and the Continental often carries top-spin from the wrist action of the player.

Top-spin drives carry a lot of heavy top-spin. The champions don't hit all such strokes in the same way for speed and top-spin. Their strokes are varied according to their needs. Such variation is best seen by comparing their passing shots from deep returns—let's say from the baseline—with crosscourt passing shots from balls taken inside (on the side nearest the net) the service line. The shot from deep has to carry speed as well as spin and so less top-spin is put on the ball. The shot close-in is hit for sharp angle and must carry heavy top-spin not only to pass the man at the net but also to stay inside the sideline.

These champions have to know what they can do with top-spin; how hard they can hit or how little they can put on the ball and still keep it in court. On their way to the top they learned from concentrated practice and experience such things as the best height at which to strike the ball for the various strokes they wish to play, and the top-spin to be used (which would be less on a dull or wet day than when sun and warmth put more bounce into the balls).

Spin is imparted to the ball by the strings of the racket as they come into contact with the ball in any way other than flat on. Diagram A shows how top-spin comes from hitting the ball in an 'up and over' motion causing the ball to rotate counterclockwise, whereas the slice and chop shots, both underslice, come from a 'down and under' racket motion to bring a clockwise rotation. The slice is also sometimes used to curve the ball to 'go away' (to the right from the righthanded forehand and the left from the righthanded backhand) and to do that the racket strokes the part of the ball closest to the player as well as 'down and under'.

34

Don't simply read this: Get out on the court and try it. It can be fun as you strike the ball at varying angles, both over and under, to see what effect they have on the ball.

If the fun goes out of that practice after a time, don't discard it. Remember that a top-spin drive is a great asset and could bring you a lot of pleasure in actual play. Remember, too, heavy top-spin takes pace off a drive and makes the ball drop from normal flight quickly. A slice tends to slow the ball and its rise. A cut ball (for the chop shot) travels faster than a sliced one, and the bound stays lower.

THE CHOP AND THE SLICE

The chop and the slice are close relatives, so close in fact that many mistake one for the other. But they are different in make and design. To chop a ball the racket face cuts across the line of flight of the bounce of the ball with a similar action to chopping wood, except that the face of the racket opens (slants back) to varying degrees depending on whether a heavy chop (which carries more speed and does not rise as high as a lightly chopped ball) is required for change of pace and/or attack, or a light chop is required mainly for a variation of pace.

The slice is made with the racket hitting under and through the ball with a clockwise turn of the wrist and hand as impact is made. This gives the ball a little runaway to the off, which is to the right when hit by a right-hander, when it lands from its flight course through the air. In this way it is used as a change of pace and 'something different' from the normal drive, and it is usually easier to control for change of length than the normal drive. Both the chop and the slice are used as disguise for drop shots with the racket passing under the ball quickly with more spin and much less follow-through, depending on the distance from the net the shot is played and the distance over the net the shot is aimed.

Both strokes can be played with either the Eastern or Continental grip with the racket held firmly and the wrist moving with a downward action for the chop and in a slight clockwise turn for the slice.

Both strokes were used more in the past than the present, and then mainly from the back of the court as a change of pace, or sometimes as a means of returning a deep and fast service when there was not time for a drive. Now the volleyer uses both strokes more as approach shots to pave his way to the net, and as a change of pace which he hopes will lead his opponent to make an error in attempting a passing shot.

35

Service

The service is the only stroke in the game with which you have two chances—a first service and a second service on each point. Also it cannot be affected by an opponent because the ball is under your control and you can do what you want with it. Make the most of these helpful circumstances.

The server in tennis is given a tremendous advantage because he is allowed to throw the ball where he wishes to contact it. Don't waste this advantage. Learn to throw up the ball for service so that you can hit it with comfort and freedom, and more importantly, with control. Learn to serve with an action that will give you racket control to use spins and twists—as well as the flat deliveries—which can confuse an opponent as well as trouble him with change of pace.

Believe me, it can be very important in your tennis life to learn a good, sound service action and be able to throw up the ball accurately for the delivery.

You don't have to be tall to serve a 'big' service, to serve aces with either speed, kick or spin. Laver is approximately 5 feet 9 inches tall, about the same height as Cliff Richey and Tony Roche and 2 inches taller than Ken Rosewall. But all serve aces, and Laver and Roche have top-spin control which they can use on service to make their second deliveries difficult for any opposition. A powerful service can 'bring you home' despite poor ground strokes, and a weak service can nullify all the fine ground strokes that server might have and never provide an opportunity to bring into action a first-rate net game.

To control the many excellent types of service used, you should grip your racket somewhere between the Eastern forehand and backhand grips, including the Continental grip. Look back to the grips I described earlier.

Before talking about the service stance and action I would caution against footfaulting, which means allowing either foot to touch any part of the baseline or the court before the ball is hit. You can jump over the line, if you wish, provided you hit the ball before landing in court. You can strike the ball for service while it is behind, or in the air inside, the baseline. Serving is like most other strokes and aspects of the game: There are many different ways of doing it well. For that reason the main thing to do when taking stance an inch or perhaps a little more behind the baseline is to make sure that you are comfortable and evenly balanced on both feet, and that as you go through the motions of striking the ball you won't have to contort your body or your arm as your weight follows through after hitting the serve. Remember too that occasionally you may wish to follow your service to the net and, therefore, your stance should help you to move on your way to the net as you follow through.

Before going further here are some of the pitfalls to avoid.

Don't stand face-on to the net or be talked into using a grip that gives only a flat service delivery, with the thought 'of changing once you find better ball control'. Far too many players never find the courage or time to practise to make a change once they have learned to hit that flat delivery into court regularly.

21 The young Australian Evonne Goolagong is the first player of aboriginal descent to reach the Top Ten of Australian tennis. This service-action photograph, illustrating slight slice on her delivery, shows she has contacted the ball at top comfortable height and just a little ahead of her body. Evonne has an easy, graceful service and, as with all her other strokes, there is a flow of weight forward into the shot.

21

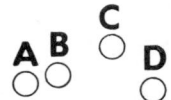

1

2

Diagram B Learning the toss-up or the throw-up of the ball for service can be dull, but it is very necessary. For a right-hander the basis of the toss-up is the left hand going up in front of the body so that the ball goes straight up and under the spot where the server wishes to contact the ball. There are often troubles ahead for the player who swings the left hand across the body so that the ball goes up and circles back to the spot where the server will strike it.

In Figure one, with the server facing out of the page, the two balls A and B are in the correct spot for a slice, with A for the wider slice to the opposition forehand. C is the position for contact for the flat service. If A, B and C were allowed to land instead of the server hitting them, they should, if tossed up correctly, drop no more than 18 inches inside the baseline, with the ball for the flat service landing a little further into the court than the ball for the slice. In other words, the server and his racket would be leaning on the ball at contact. Ball D is lower and more to the left for the racket—after being down behind the back—to come up behind the head, brushing the strings firmly upward and roughly over the ball. It imparts the necessary spin, in conjunction with the power of the racket action, to make a kicking service. In this figure, C could also be hit for a slice by using more 'racket work' on the ball. However, the slice imparted in such a case would be less than that on A and B.

In the second figure we have the back view of a server who bends his body sideways as he tries to strike the ball comfortably at his top height. In this case the toss-up for the slice is C and not so far to the right. The flat service contacts the ball almost as a straight line from the left leg upwards, and the kicker toss-up is again lower than the others and to the left. Try to avoid any service action which places great strain on the shoulder, neck, arm, or stomach muscles. Experiment with the toss-up to find what suits you best.

Diagram C Position of feet for serving

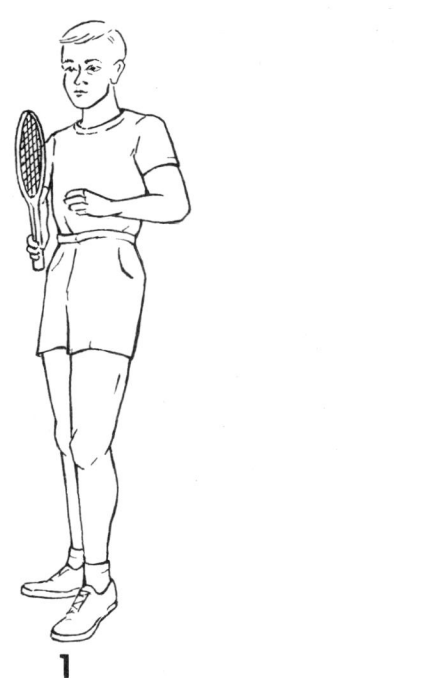

1   **2**

Don't throw the ball up too high, because it might lead to your having to break the much sought-after rhythm of your service action.

Don't throw the ball up with an arm action that will take the ball in a swinging motion until it is in the correct place to be hit, especially when it is easy to learn to throw the ball up with your arm in front of your body.

Finally, don't throw away your first delivery by trying to hit it at an impossible speed, with the chance of getting only a few percent of serves into play.

Let us begin with the service action by repeating that it is very important to develop rhythm. Judging by the many different but very fine services and service actions I have seen among champions, it is impossible to lay down any hard and fast rules about the angles of the feet in relation to the baseline, the direction in which the racket or the shoulders should be pointing as the service is started, the distance between the feet or how best to use the weight of your body.

22   23

Until recent years it was customary to hold two or three balls in your hand when beginning to serve (three in case one was a 'let'). Nowadays many players hold only one ball and keep another in a pocket. If there is a 'let' call on a first service and then a fault, they simply call for another ball. Some players don't like to change from the two-balls-in-the-hand, for if there is some hitch in getting the ball out of the pocket or they have to call for a ball when there is a 'let' on the first service, they believe they lose the benefit of knowing what went wrong with their first delivery.

The stance is approximately half-side-on to the net and for many deliveries the server is actually facing in the direction of the net post (if he is a righthander). This changes slightly depending on the type of serve to be delivered. For instance, the feet for a service, almost flat or with medium slice, into the first court are usually positioned as in diagram C (1), but they often change to (2) when they serve a kicking delivery to the backhand into the second court.

The feet should be far enough apart to be comfortable and to allow for a slight movement of weight backwards and then forwards as the arm, shoulder and bodyweight go forward into the service. The feet should be approximately 10 to 24 inches apart, usually according to one's height.

40

22, 23, 24 Bill Durham's throwing action here can be likened to his service action (see pictures 25–29)

The racket is normally held about lower-chest level and in front, the free hand with the ball or balls resting against some part of the racket. The racket is usually held with its head high.

From this point on you must seek rhythm and synchronization of the right and left hands so that the ball will reach the point of contact with the racket at the top of the throw-up and after the racket has completed its motion of down, up, a drop behind the head, and finally, the last sweep up to contact the ball, usually slightly in front of and above the server's head. Take a good long look at the serving sequences. It is important to understand what happens. I repeat that you must try to acquire rhythm in your service.

Playing at the position of the stance, I want to go on from there with the service action. First let me draw your attention to that throwing action you see in pictures 22, 23 and 24. Serving is similar, and the main difference is that the shoulder and arm stretch higher so that, when the ball is contacted on a normal flat or slightly sliced service, the player is reaching—with comfort—to strike the ball in the middle of the racket as high up as possible. Your stance is relaxed. Remember that the ball is to go above and in front—perhaps above the right eye rather than the left eye, to be explicit—

25   26   27

25–29 Bill Durham started this service delivery standing evenly balanced and with his left hand holding two balls resting at about where the balance-point of his racket and the end of the sleeve of his left arm are in diagram C. The motion begins with both the hand with the balls and the racket-hand going down, as illustrated in picture 25, and then starting up. In picture 26, the ball

and that you must allow your arm, shoulder and weight to follow through with the racket.

Now, as the right hand swings the racket down close to the knees and the ground, the left hand also drops. Usually the knees bend slightly with the action. Then, as the racket begins its upward action—with the wrist loose—to reach slightly higher than the back of the head before going down behind the middle of the back, the left hand moves upward to take the ball in the hand to approximately top-of-the-head high. The ideal is to

42

28   **29**

has gone up (not as high as it appears from the angle at which this picture was taken) and in 27 the racket is about to begin a very rapid movement, with tremendous wrist work, down behind the head and then up and into the ball (picture 28) with Bill's weight, having gone into the service, carrying him through as he is on his way to the net hoping for a 'put away' volley or smash.

have the hand move directly up to where you wish to contact the ball (above the right eye, we decided for this service). Then the swing upward— the final swing upward—of the racket from the middle of the back begins as the ball is released from the hand, and the action of the racket from that moment is so fast that it meets the ball, hopefully, as the ball reaches the desired height in front of and above the head. This final surge upward is very fast and much of the speed of the service comes from that last split-second gathering of speed of the racket head.

43

In the racket head's last upward surge the shoulder and arm reach up and the body weight moves forward as if all the server's power was being drawn from the feet up through the arms and hands into the racket. Power is needed, for this is the one stroke in the game in which the ball has no usable momentum from the opponent—unlike volleying a fast drive, when you can simply block the shot and direct the ball with the racket. But the serving power must be controlled.

You can see from pictures 25 to 33 that there is a full circular action of the racket head behind the server's back. It appears a little more difficult than it is. For those who know this loose-wristed swing, the path of the racket is almost automatic. To return to the throwing-up of the ball: If you have trouble in timing your swing to contact the ball at the top of the throw by reaching up comfortably, then either slow or quicken the racket swing at the beginning of the whole action, with the hand holding the balls either higher or lower on the racket. It is most important to synchronize the throw and the swing, not only in order to contact the ball as high as comfortably possible, but also to find a rhythm in your service action which will bring consistency and accuracy.

Stance, throw-up, racket swing, direction of body weight and speed of racket movement all have bearing on what type of service is delivered. However, the most important factor is the angle of the face of the racket as it strikes the ball—flat, with side-spin or top-spin. The most common of these is the side-spin which is usually known as the slice service. As the ball is struck the racket strings impart a little clockwise spin to the ball and the finish of the stroke takes the racket across the front of the server's body to his left side. Greater spin would take the finish of the stroke more to the left. In contrast, the flat service would finish with the racket head close to the body; some players take it close to the left side and others very close to the right side.

The throw-up you should have for service is in picture 34 of Adi Kourim, and the one you don't want is the dotted line which takes the ball up in a wide arc, because it brings a wide margin of error into your chance of putting the ball where you want it for different services. Although you *must* practise the throw-up, you should also practise every part of the service. It is so easy to practise: you can do it by yourself—throw-up, racket swing, weight going up and into the service, eye always on the ball, putting what 'work' you wish on the ball for spin or anything else, and the back foot swinging forward and over the base line (but not touching the ground before you strike the ball) as you move forward toward the net.

44

Return of service

It is well recognized that the server has a major advantage. So, what to do about it? Much can be done to minimize that advantage and, in the order that you should be thinking about such measures as your opponent serves, here they are:

1. An overwhelming majority of players have a pattern of service, and few change that pattern because (a) they have no other serves and (b) they don't give the game sufficient tactical thought. Therefore, try to remember what type of service your opponent usually delivers and prepare for it by thinking of the best service replies.

2. Try to get into the habit of 'reading' what the serve will do with the ball (has your opponent's service action been for slice, kick, etc.?) and anticipating the direction of the serve as early as possible after it leaves the racket.

3. If you know the first service is to be fast, it is perhaps advisable to stand well back, perhaps a little behind the baseline. But don't take a baseline stance awaiting service if you know the service will be short—and of course this is particularly important regarding a second service. If you are standing in (nearer the net) to receive a slow or short service it is so much easier to take the ball on the rise or at the top of the bound and attack than if you have to make a late run in towards it from the baseline or from further back.

4. Attack the service if you can. I have seen players attack a ball in a backcourt rally when it landed two or three yards inside the baseline, yet play almost defensively a short service much closer to the net and just as easy to get at.

5. Remember that if your opponent is following in toward the net after service, the earlier you strike the ball the less distance he will have covered in approaching the net, and therefore you will have greater opportunity to score with a passing shot.

6. The direction of the return of service must depend, first, on your ability to make various shots, and secondly, on the server's approach to the net and his ability to play various strokes. Some dislike the low, direct return to their feet, preferring that same shot where they reach to the side for it.

30   **31**   **32**

30–33 The first picture here shows the middle of the backswing of Adi Kourim's service. This would be the same as picture 27 in Bill Durham's service. Now fit pictures 31, 32 and 33 of Kourim's service (with 33 showing contact with the ball) in between pictures 27 and 28 of Durham's service, and you will see the complete picture of the swing behind the head and back before the racket finally goes up and above the head to strike the ball.

Some play the waist-high returns confidently but falter badly on the head-high volleys. Many who follow to the net have poor balance and stroke control if they have to move out of their line of approach to the net, and against these you must sometimes play down-the-line shots.

7. If your opponent remains at the back of the court, don't fall into the habit of returning everything to the baseline. It is a misunderstanding to regard hitting to the baseline as good length. It is poor length if your

46

33

34, 35 The throw-up for service. This service action of Adi Kourim shows two excellent examples of fundamentals: The first is carelessness in that he has allowed his foot to stray onto the line before striking the ball; the second is that his throw-up of the ball is perfect for his fast, flat and slightly swinging type of serve. He likes to have his weight moving forward as he strikes the ball about 18 inches inside the area above the baseline.

34

35

opponent has no intention of going to the net and has stayed back after service. A much better return of service would be a deceptive drop shot, a sharp angle or a shot into one of the backcourt corners, depending on which side found an opposition weakness or which side was being guarded more closely.

8. Don't become a 'habit' returner of service in doubles. Watch a few games and you will see at first-hand that it is possible to watch a complete

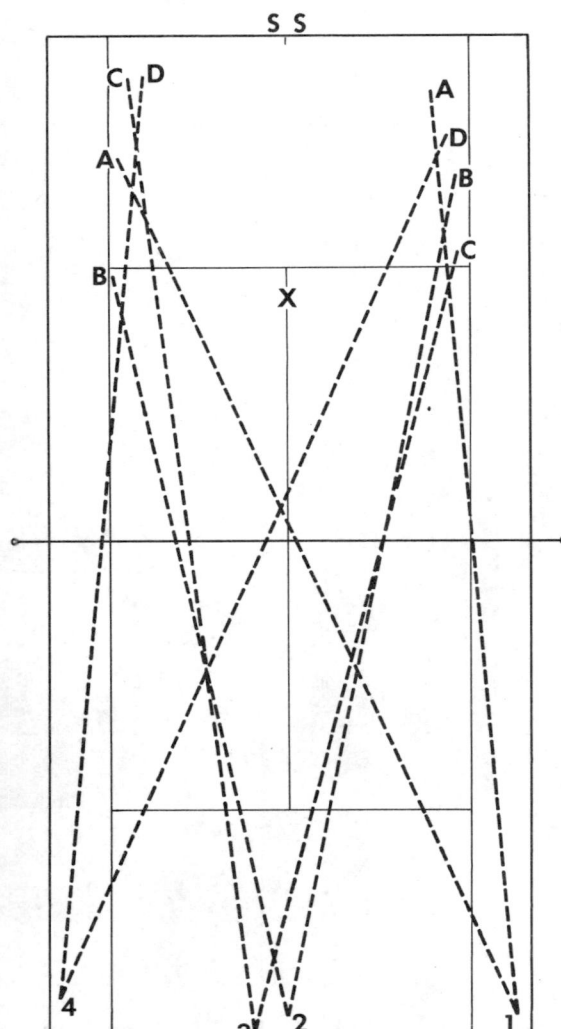

Diagram D This diagram shows only the returns of service. You must imagine that the server has placed his services to points 1, 2, 3 and 4, 1 and 2 being to the forehand, wide and down the centre of the first court, and 3 and 4 down the centre and wide to the second court. I have taken it for granted that the server has moved in toward the net to, let's say, X, and so the returns of service shown are made to beat the approaching server. However, they would also be excellent returns if the server were to remain back on the baseline. The diagram shows 1, 2, 3 and 4 returns going to A, B, C and D respectively. There is no need to return the ball to the server, yet this is the common practice at most levels of play.

set and see every—repeat every—return of service hit back (whether over or into the net does not matter here) in the direction of the server, and aimed back to the server if the serve is not followed to the net. It seems unbelievable that not once in a set has the return been angled differently—that it has not been whacked down someone's line, or dropped just over the net if the server remains back, or chipped back, chopped back or sliced back for a change of pace, or lobbed back.

48

The most obvious and oft-repeated tactical mistake among young players and beginners is to stand in the same place to receive service, regardless of the power, speed or spin of the delivery and of whether it is first or second service.

I have seen a higher percentage of young players and beginners in America than in any other well-developed tennis-playing country standing a yard or two behind the baseline as a matter of course when receiving service, and even further back behind the baseline when rallying.

Two yards behind the baseline would be too far to stand even if the servers they opposed could send down cannonball deliveries. But of course in that level of competition there are no cannonball services.

The main reasons why standing a yard or more behind the baseline is poor tactics are:

1. The further one is back from the net the more difficult it is to hit winners, and it is hard for a player of any level to hit a winner from two yards behind the baseline against a player of comparable standard.

2. The additional time it takes for the ball to travel the extra four yards (two beyond and two back to the baseline) can make the difference between a net-rusher being in a defensive volleying position and a winning one.

3. It is almost impossible for anyone but a first-class player from a yard or two yards behind the baseline to reach a good drop shot or drop volley and make an effective stroke.

4. It is not possible for most youngsters to reach even a mid-court ball and play it well when starting to run from two yards behind the baseline.

A young player and a beginner must be taught to receive no further back than the baseline. It would have to be an exceptional service for a young player to force another youngster to go further back.

Most services at that age and class level should be taken earlier, and youngsters should be taught to move in toward the net for a second service if they note a certain player's second serve is usually short, and in some cases they could move in almost to the service line.

To allow them to learn to stand behind the baseline is almost encouraging flat-footedness, lack of thought, a slow get-'em-all-back spirit and a negative attitude to quick thinking during play.

Volley

When you go to the net to volley, it should be to end the point. You won't win with what many miscall good-length volleys close to the baseline. Too many players can 'cover' almost anything baseline-deep, unless a previous shot has taken them wide out of court. Use your volleys deceptively to catch an opponent on the wrong foot; make him struggle to reach a stop volley or drop volley; force him to stretch wide for a short or long angle. Make all this easier by playing in close to the net until your opponent sends a lob over your head—sometimes, you know, opponents don't even think of that. And remember: use the initial speed of your opponent's shot by blocking or short-punching your volleys. There is no need for a long swing at a volley.

I began playing tennis when I was thirteen and shortly afterwards heard the tennis maxim that the perfect baseliner will always beat the perfect net-rusher. The logic there is that no one can cover all the net in singles as well as the perfect lob to the baseline, whereas the baseliner can cover his side of the court because he has more time to play his strokes. The closer I got to top tennis the clearer this fact became. It was brought home to me many times when I was passed at the net after failing to put volleying chances away for winners.

The volley is almost always referred to as an attacking shot. Sometimes, however, the player who wants to get to the net, after service especially and sometimes during a rally, finds the opposition's return so good that the first volley is defensive. Then placement is more important than power so the volleyer can continue to move closer to the net to take up a better attacking position for the next chance to volley.

On that first defensive volley a favourite tennis slogan for volleying, 'never let your racket head fall below your wrist level', should be broken unless the player moving in toward the net has agility above the ordinary and can move forward easily in a crouched position. For most people it is almost physically impossible to keep the head of the racket above the wrist on the very low volleys and half-volleys without stopping. On the other hand, most good players can continue to advance to the net while bending the knees in order to get partially down to the low ball and to play

50

it with the head of the racket down. If the return looks extremely difficult it will pay to stop and get right down to it, but otherwise the head-below-the-wrist volley can be most effective.

Attacking volleys can be made from the baseline. Often there is a volleying opportunity off a deep drive. Instead of stepping back to allow the ball to land close to the baseline, step forward and volley it with a firm grip. It is much easier to play than it may sound, and such a stroke has a tremendous advantage over a drive in that it will often find the opposition still out of good court position after playing the previous shot. If that is the case, the point can be pressed home more vigorously by going to the net because the movement to volley the ball has become the first step on the way to the net.

Anything other than a low defensive volley or a half-volley should be played with either power or placement or both. In thinking of placement I mention the stop volley and the drop volley, which serve the same purpose, are alike yet different.

The drop volley is made by allowing the racket to fall slightly back and away from the ball—and along the same flight—at the moment of impact. The racket forms a 'cushion' to take the pace off the ball which then falls softly and short over the net.

The stop volley is different in execution but played for the same effect. It is made by turning the wrist slightly clockwise on the forehand and counterclockwise on the backhand at the moment of impact. This puts back-spin on the ball and keeps it and the bounce short—you hope—just over the net. This takes practice, but so does every other stroke if you want to do it well. As your confidence in this drop volley increases you can try to angle the shot at the same time as putting on the back-spin. Done well, this can give you great satisfaction, but I repeat that it takes much practice to do well. You can tell from the action pictures of Adi Kourim (see pictures 36, 37) that he has turned his body sideways as he approached the net and judged that the return would come high to his backhand volley. This position will give him a similar stroking action to his forehand volley, which to most players is the more natural stroke. It will give him power as well as position to place the ball down the line or across court.

Adi's footwork in that stroke is correct. When volleying, if there is time, the footwork should be similar to that used for driving, so here he assumed a sideways position to the net with his feet and with the outside of his right shoulder facing in the direction of the ball. If it had been a forehand volley about the same height, the left shoulder would have turned in the direction

36—37 Adi Kourim is perfectly balanced as he plays this backhand volley. Note his 'eye on the ball'

of the ball, but not as far.

Often, however, there won't be time to worry about footwork. The majority of volleys in singles, and even more in doubles, are taken so quickly that all one can do is get the racket to the ball and use body weight going onto the foot nearest the ball, plus strength from the forearm and a firm grip of the racket.

The forehand side is the easiest side to position quickly for power on this rapidly executed volley, and a pivot of the top of the body from the hips counterclockwise will give some shoulder- and more arm-power to the backhand side.

The most common error in volleying is taking a long swing for it. There is usually no time for anything but a short punch and much of the pace of your volley will come from the pace of your opponent's shot. Often your volley in close duels will be nothing other than a stiff-wristed block. Because of the speed of volleying it is easy to take your eye off the ball, when in fact you should watch the ball even more closely—if that were possible—than for other strokes.

One further hint: Don't always practise volleying standing close to the net. You should practise just as much from the service line because that is where you will play many volleys and from that position you will probably need more practice than closer to the net to make satisfying shots.

HALF-VOLLEY

The half-volley is usually the most difficult shot in the game.

If you wish to half-volley well I advise knee-bending exercises each morning and night. You must 'get down' to half-volleys whether you play them where they are most valuable (that is, moving in toward the net) or whether you play them from the back of the court when time or position does not allow some other stroke with less risk factor.

The main reasons why the half-volley is the most difficult stroke for most players are (a) that they don't bend their knees and get down to the ball; (b) that they drop their racket down almost perpendicularly to it instead of getting down early and sweeping toward the ball at a low level; and (c) that they don't watch the ball closely enough, which means right onto the racket.

Too often the inexperienced player will hit a half-volley a few yards from the net with the same power as a full drive. The only chance such a shot would have of going over the net and landing in the opponent's court would be to have it hit the top of the net to slow it up and then drop over as a net-cord shot. You can practise the half-volley by standing at about the service line and have someone volley the ball down to hit the court around your feet and a little wide of you.

Speedy racket movement is essential to good volleying, especially in doubles when at times all four players are at the net exchanging rapid-fire volleys. You can improve your volleying and particularly the quick volleying by practising them. Have someone hit the balls at you from varying distances and at various speeds. You might be scared of some of the fast ones but the fright quickly disappears as you 'get onto' one or two of those fast shots and volley them back. If you have no companion to hit balls to you, practise against a wall by standing close; but have a number of balls to practise with to save time ballboying for yourself. There will be many more misses than hits in the early days of such practice.

38

39

42

43

40   41

38–43 The Wimbledon champion of 1953 and the American champion of 1954, Vic Seixas is seen in this fine action-study of good balance, eye-on-the-ball, and most important, of a half volley being made not by suddenly dropping the racket down at a ball as most beginners do. Instead, as Vic shows in this sequence taken at Wimbledon, it should be made by getting the racket well behind the flight of the ball, and meeting it, you might say, 'squarely', and not trying to 'hit the cover off it'—as you can see by the stroke's short follow-through.

44

44 Few beginners realize that in a normal service action the racket falls as far behind the back as Mary Dana Livingston has it here for the final sweep upward to contact the ball

45 Mary Dana Livingston is meeting the ball beautifully here for a high forehand volley

45

46

47

46, 47 The left foot is forward so that when Mary Dana Livingston puts her weight into her forehand drive and her racket follows through, as in 47, she has good balance for fast recovery to move anywhere her opponent's shot may go

48 I am showing Mary Dana Livingston here how much of the strength for power in a very high backhand volley or a backhand smash comes from the forearm. She is using a slightly shortened racket grip, believing it will give her more control over her racket and therefore over her stroke

48

Lob

It is better to lob some balls out and some deep in court rather than give your opponent confidence from hitting easy winners from short lobs.

The lob is basically defensive, but it can be turned to attack. It is one of the most neglected strokes of the game, and even those who use it seldom practise it for any time commensurate with its value. In every era of the game since I first played internationally in 1927 I have found some of the champions who could attack with their lobs against destructive net-rushers, and I think immediately of Rod Laver with his lefthanded top-spin lob and Ken Rosewall with his very deceptive righthanded slightly under-sliced lob. The top-spin, the sliced and the flat or driving lob are the ones we see in every tournament of top status. There is another, the reverse top-spin—hit with the same face of the racket used for the drive—and rarely used.

You must understand spin before you try the top-spin lob. The ball is hit with the same type of top-spin used to drive top-spin but the spin is generally much heavier. In other words, more spin is necessary for this lob than for a drive. A tremendous amount of wrist action is necessary, and the ball when struck begins in a high arc to go over the head of the net player by a small margin and then, when it lands—rather suddenly and sharply—'runs away' quickly from the player trying to retrieve it. This lob is enhanced when players can begin it with the same backswing as a top-spin drive and so bring deception to their shot.

The heavy top-spin on this lob makes it difficult for some to smash. It means that sometimes even a mediocre top-spin lob is missed by a player who fails to 'get over' the ball with plenty of loose-wristed swing to 'counter' the heavy top-spin.

The slice lob explains itself. The ball is controlled with slice, letting the face of the racket open slightly just before impact—depending on the height wanted on the lob—with the wrist moving counter-clockwise about the same degree as the racket face. There is not as much pace on the ball as on the top-spun lob and the slice imparted appears to 'hold the ball in the air'. It is used often these days by many top players to 'float' a ball down-the-line over the backhand smash side of the opposition, but its

58

main use comes with its deception in changing what may start out as a drive for a passing shot into a lob as the net player moves forward in anticipation of the drive.

The drive or flat lob is also used in attack as well as defence. Perhaps the best example comes from the forehand side when the play is as you see in diagram E. The player at the baseline has played a short return from A to B and moves toward C to protect his forehand court. The net player has angled the ball across to D and moves toward the centre or a little to his left of centre to cover a down-the-line shot toward E. It is then that the baseliner suddenly turns his drive into a lob over the net man's head to F.

This tactic can be repeated from the backhand side, and of course both are great for doubles where lobbing is more often seen because two men at the net each have less expanse of the net to cover (two covering 36 feet) than a singles player with 27 feet to cover, while the length of the court is the same—38 feet from net to baseline.

The slice lob is used defensively by lobbing a little higher than when making an attacking lob, but the most-used defensive lob is the flat lob, often blocked back rather than stroked back, from an opposition smash or a big service too difficult to hit as a reasonably effective driving return of service. High defensive lobbing must sometimes be changed. For instance there are some players who are deadly with a high lob which they allow to land and then smash. To such players that defensive lob must be lower but deep.

In good tennis lobs must be deep. Most top players can 'put away' any lob they can contact between the net and the service line on their forehand side, and a lob down the backhand line must be fairly low to be fast enough to prevent most players running around it to take it on their forehand smash.

Don't forget that the crosscourt lob has much more court length in which to fall than the straight lob. Get out your geometry book and work it out for yourself so you will remember the advantage the lob gives you.

Other uses for the lob are:
1. To change the pace of a game in the hope of unsettling an opponent.
2. When you think your opponent is tired but continues to attack to shorten the rallies.
3. Obviously, when you know your opponent cannot smash.
4. When you believe your opponent cannot handle a high ball on the backhand, you can lob to that corner and follow it to the net.
5. When your opponent is facing the sun and a good lob will give him an

'eye-full'. There is nothing unsportsmanlike in that. If your opponent does not handle that sun, he can stay back. He does *not* have to go to the net.

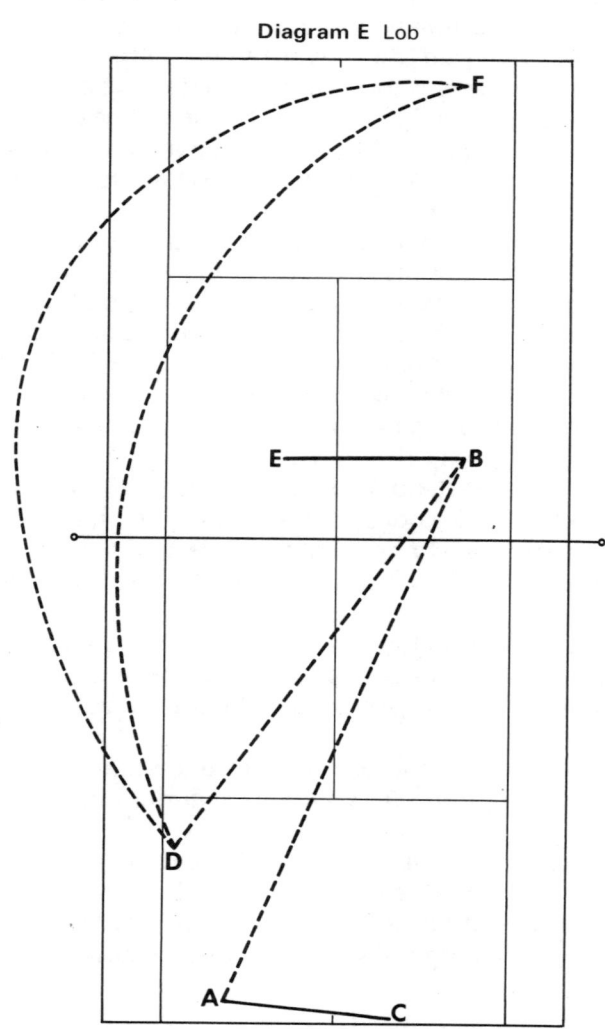

Diagram E Lob

Smash

If you cannot smash effectively, you might as well give up going to the net to volley against a tactical opponent, because the volleyer who cannot smash effectively stays so far back from the net to protect his smash (or overhead) that his volleying is no longer effective.

There is an axiom which says, 'As you serve so you shall smash', and it should be true to tennis form because most players use the same grip and swing for the overhead balls as for the service.

The smash must be practised. It is important to be confident with the smash because a tentative overhead against someone wise enough to detect lack of confidence and who can also lob will weaken even the strongest, fittest and fastest players. It must be hit with confidence because it should be aggressive in placement as well as speed.

Where most players require smashing practice is not so much in the stroke itself but in the movement back from the net from the volleying position—movement fast enough to get under a lob which might hit the baseline, and movement so well controlled as to allow the smasher to get off the ground and into the air to strike the ball.

If you normally smash well but begin a match by missing some, don't move back a long way to make sure of 'covering' the next lob. In moving back it gives the opponent greater angles to 'make' with passing shots and that means the 'next lob' might never come.

The moment you sense your opponent about to lob or you see the ball going up you must begin to move backward. Avoid falling into the habit of using a lot of small shuffling steps, and try to get used to your first step being a long backward stride. With most people this is a step with the right foot, and it may be so with you too. Practice will tell. Once you are on the way you will learn to judge what small quick steps might be necessary to take you up to striking the ball, naturally well above your head and slightly in front. There is much wrist movement in the smash and this should be accentuated when smashing a top-spin lob; the extra wrist action nullifies some of the spin. You may have to turn your body—or at least your shoulders—as you begin to go back for the smash. This also you will do best after intensive practice. Don't

49

49 Tony Roche leaps off the ground for an overhead with his eye on the ball; he is about halfway through his swing to smash the ball. When Tony completes the stroke and is back on the court surface he will instinctively move in towards the net again. John Newcombe moves back with Tony and watches his partner closely because, if Tony's smash is a good one, John will move in fast (while Tony is recovering) in the hope of 'picking off' a weak return close in at the net. A good doubles team moves together when possible—either back to the baseline or, preferably, up to the net.

50 This picture of the finish of a smash is interesting because it shows how the wrist and racket have turned slightly 'outwards' as the girl has played for an angle. The racket follow-through will finish down on her right side. If the smash had been crosscourt to a right-hander's forehand, the racket would have finished down on the left side of the body.

50

51 This is *not* a gimmick. It is a very simple method of showing players at any level the court they can 'find' with shots where the ball is struck above their eyes. It is instructive in the use of any type of shot, whether the ball is hit flat or with some form of spin, but of course, the direct eye-to-court look relates to the flat-hit shot. Here one of America's young prospects, Billy Martin of River Forest, Illinois, whose performances rate him the best fourteen-year-old in the U.S., is learning for the first time the tremendous angles in one with a good overhead (smash) can hit from the centre of the court. Before Billy climbed the umpire's stand he swung as if to contact an overhead and I am holding the racket at that height. He has put his face almost against the racket so that he is looking through it at about the spot where he would have hoped to strike the ball. The umpire's stand should be moved to other parts of the court and other smashing angles studied. This is a fine method, too, of showing players the margins they have with flat services, and is an important way of stressing to short players why they must not try too often for the exhilarating 'big flat ace' and why they must rely on spin. The above procedure has also proved very fruitful in stopping youngsters from smashing almost everything back to the baseline. Angle smashing is a must for every player.

51

always smash straight down the centre of the court or either crosscourt or to-the-off (which is to the backhand—left court—corner). It is comparatively easy to learn to smash in all directions either with arm and wrist action or by slight turning of the upper body. A smash always in the one spot can be disastrous unless it carries unusual speed.

Keep in mind that the player with faith in his being able to 'cover' almost anything in the air usually volleys better than most because he has the confidence to move in close to the net where the best volleying work is done. If you have tried to get up into the air for your smashes and have failed, don't despair. There are many champions who can smash decisively while keeping one foot firmly on the ground. Experimenting is the only way to learn which is best for you.

The backhand smash is seldom hit with similar freedom. Some players never use it. They try to cover everything with the forehand smash, and if they cannot cover a lob wide to the backhand side they prefer to let the ball land and then treat it as a high drive or lob it back.

The champions, however, mostly play a quiet placement stroke on that backhand smashing side, hitting the ball with much less freedom and power and often using the wrist a great deal in an effort to make a placement or to hit the ball deep to give themselves time to recover good court position. They do that in preference to relinquishing the net position by allowing the ball to land. Some play that backhand smash with confidence and sound control, but to most it is a very difficult stroke.

Drop shot

One of the most pleasing tactics of the game of tennis, especially if you are playing it successfully and it is disrupting your opponent's game, is the drop-shot-and-lob tactic which brings the opponent scrambling in to reach the drop shot and then sends him scurrying back for a low lob or lob volley, which lands somewhere close to the baseline.

The drop shot is the ball played to land just over the net, when an opponent is close to the baseline, in the hope that it will be a winner. It is closely related to the drop volley. It is a delicate stroke, one which requires perfect timing and, in most cases if it is to succeed, some deception.

The usual way to play it is to begin the stroke as if playing a slice or a chop shot and then, just before contact with the ball, open the face of the racket and slow up the stroke action so that the ball will go only just over the net and the bound will be short. In doing this, off forehand or backhand, the wrist must turn slightly—clockwise for forehand and counterclockwise for backhand—at the moment of impact. That wrist movement and the fact that the drop shot must be short over the net means that there is a great risk factor in it and it therefore requires much practice. It requires even more practice if one plays a back-spinning drop shot because the back-spin, put on the ball to stop the bounce short or even to bring it back closer to the net, requires more and faster wrist movement.

If you wish to learn it, practise it a lot. A poor drop shot is dangerous. In the first place the drop shot is generally played off a shot which could also be driven, and so a point which might have been won some other way is lost if the ball fails to reach the net; and secondly, if the timing is poor and the drop has no surprise element and goes over the net too far, it turns the point into a fairly easy kill for the opponent.

Don't try to win with drop shots from the back of the court. Play one from near the baseline and note how long it takes to go over the net. I am sure you will agree that it takes longer than most opponents would take to run from the back of the court to be in good position to play it.

The best drop shot is usually played off a short return which your opponent expects you to hit with pace. The speed at which your opponent

52

can run forward will decide from what distance back from the net you can afford to play a drop shot. Some players move well across the baseline, but slowly when moving forward or backward. In this respect the drop shot can be used effectively to break up the backcourt accuracy of some opponents, and even more effectively against a baseliner who does not like to play the net or perhaps cannot smash well. Then the drop is used to bring the opponent to the net, and if it is returned, a lob is used to send the player back. This tactic can test an opponent's stamina as well as win points.

Diagram F Here B had hit a short ball to A. A runs to it and begins what to B should appear as a forehand drive. Just before ball contact, however, A decides to play a drop shot. I have designated three places at which he might aim. Of course, he could have tried to play it closer to the net (the closer, i.e. the shorter, the better) or closer to each of the sidelines. Where he would decide to play would depend to a degree on what direction B was moving in in anticipation of the drive A started out to make.

Because it is a low-through-the-air shot, the drop shot should not be attempted from too far back in court unless the opposition is very slow. A badly-made drop shot means trouble for the maker.

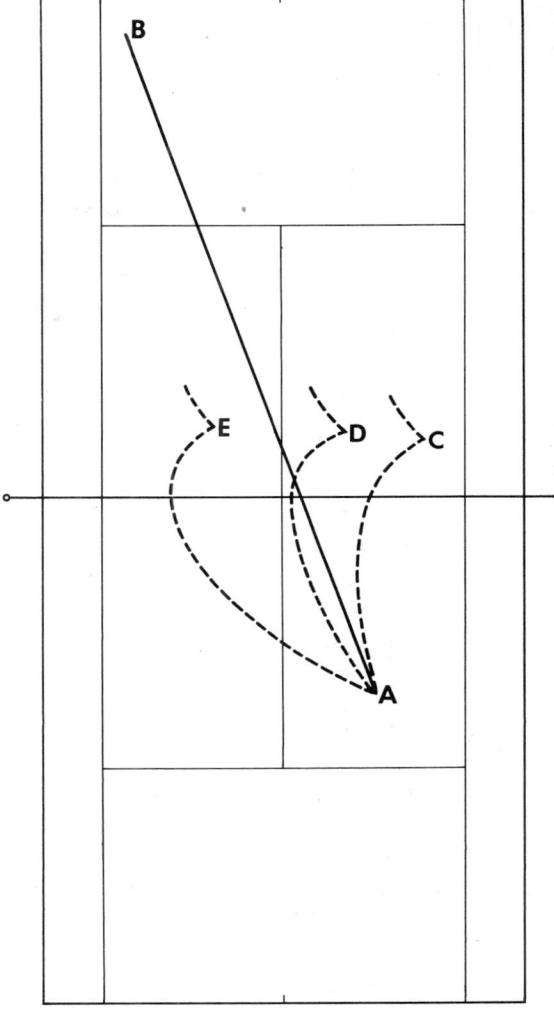

If you happen to be the player who does not move forward and backward well and also cannot smash well, often the best reply to the drop shot—if you reach it—is to redrop it and perhaps catch your opponent unawares. Don't overplay the drop. Remember that your opponent should be 'caught' with it; once he expects a drop shot he gets a flying start to reach it. The slower the court the better the drop shot—a damp or heavily grassed court or a slow, porous, brick-dust type of hard court is best. The drop shot is very common in Europe, which has only the latter type of court.

Tactics

I am a believer in attack. Here, however, I want to talk about one move toward the net that I often notice in junior play where I am sure the player would reap a greater success by retreating. (See diagram G.)

A player is forced to either the forehand or backhand sideline, short of the service line, and with the bounce taking the player outside the sideline. He decides to hit deep to mid-court (for my purpose I could say deep to the backhand or the forehand corner) and, because he is halfway to the net, decides to continue in to B, hoping to receive a ball he can volley or, a long-shot chance, hoping that his rush to the net will lead to an opposition error.

The alternatives to moving in closer to the net are (a) to take the shortest route to the centre of the court position, which would mean volleying perhaps defensively from about the service line C, and (b) retreating to the backcourt D, which would be the longest distance to run if the opponent's reply was deep to the backhand corner E. The longer flight of the ball and its bounce would give more time to play the ball and there would be much less risk of losing the point.

In diagram G you can see the amount of court you would have to cover very rapidly to intercept on the volley the anticipated shot to the backhand corner. That is not the only worry, of course. Your opponent has the alternatives of driving into the forehand corner if he thinks you might be moving fast enough to make the interception, and he has the lob, preferably to the forehand corner.

Because of that alternative to the lob I would prefer A to move to the centre of the court in the hope of making a defensive volley; his risk factor is cut down because the distance is less and, therefore, he can move back toward his forehand sideline if caught wrong-footed, and a lob over his head would be too risky to try.

Diagram H shows the alternative I prefer in this situation. If the drive is a yard or two short of the baseline, A would run to C but, if the ball hit within a foot or so of the baseline, A must run to the expected top of the bounce, maybe two yards behind the baseline.

A should run the first several strides headed that way, but then turn

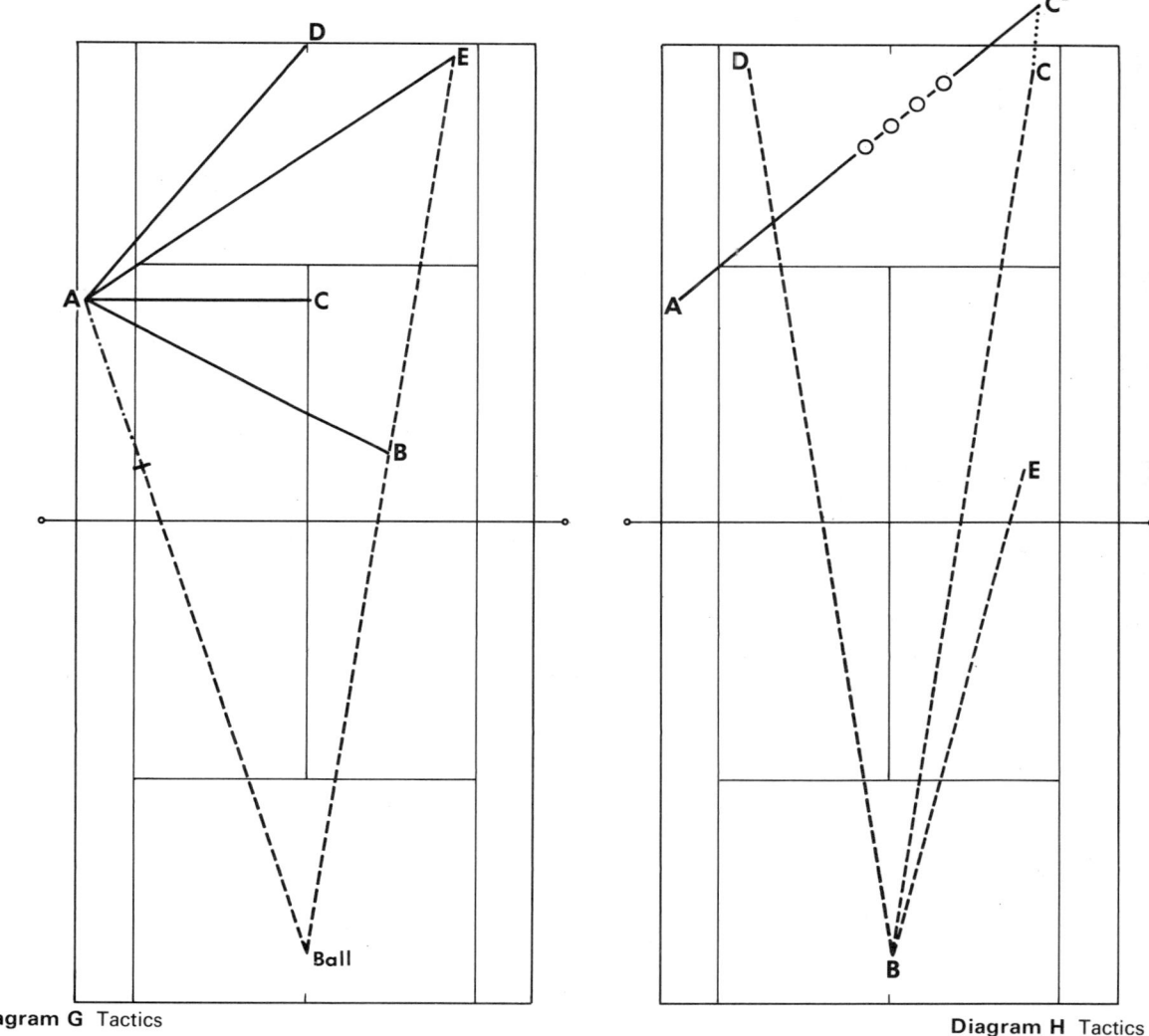

Diagram G Tactics

Diagram H Tactics

and skip sideways to watch what B is doing, in case he decides to try to catch A wrong-footed by driving into the forehand corner to D, or drop-shotting to E. If the shot heads for C then turn and run hard, deciding as you go whether to 'go for' a winning drive or to play safe with a high lob which would give you time, while it is in the air, to recover good court position—and some air in the lungs.

69

LEARN TO SKIP SIDEWAYS

If skipping sideways as you move to a ball is something new to you, you *must* learn it quickly. It is an essential to backcourt play because you *must* watch where your stroke took the ball and what your opponent is doing. The follow-through of most strokes of the majority of champions pulls them around from a side-on-to-the-net position to be facing the net once again, as you can see in the strip shown of Rod Laver bouncing in his sideways skipping action after completing the follow-through of a lefthanded, backhand drive and once again facing the net and ready to skip sideways into position (see pictures 53, 54, 55). You will see the champions making these skip steps frequently as they judge from some yards off what steps they need to arrive with feet in the best position for balance as they strike the ball; as they move forward into attack and try to position their body to allow easy and free movement of the volleying arm; as they move back for a smash and just before jumping for the ball, they try to have the right foot in the correct position to gain spring to where they wish to strike the ball. Such 'dancing' movements become so much part of their game they would be a little surprised if told they had 'danced about the court'.

53

54

53, 54, 55
Skipping sideways

55

Think

The art of lawn tennis
Is control and restraint
And putting the ball
Where the other guy ain't.

The most obvious and the most frequent mistake in play among the youngsters of all levels who attended my Summer Coaching Camp at Amherst College, USA, in 1970 and 1971, was the big hit off a short-ball—often hit out—when a quiet placement just over the net would have won the point. The desire to hit a 'big one', to whack a winner, to 'kill' the ball, comes to most tennis players at times and often must be restrained. It happens in everyday-life and in sport—as one grows older the quietly executed business coup, or the well-controlled placement which leaves the opponent stranded, brings greater satisfaction than the 'showy' action.

You must curb any desire to hit everything with power. Rod Laver can hit a high backhand volley as hard as most players can hit a service, but he often plays this stroke for a quiet angled volley winner. I have watched an occasional match where a young player has hit every first service with power—and either into the net or out—and then soft-pedalled a second service which almost asked to be returned for a winner. How foolish it looked! How much better it would have been to slow down that first serve until range had been found, until rhythm had returned, and then gradually to increase its speed. In the case above it may not have been necessary to increase the speed of that first service. A medium-paced service might have been producing winning results, and if so should not be changed except occasionally for variety. When I was playing top international tennis and my reflexes were fast, I preferred to receive a fast service (within reason, of course, and not an explosive delivery) to a slow-kicking delivery to my backhand, especially on a slow court like the slow hard courts of Europe. I found I had to make a full stroke with power to generate pace off a slow high-kicker, and in going for that pace I made more errors than in blocking back or half-stroking the flat, fast service.

In other words, you must *think* about your game and use what you have to get the best possible results.

72

In every tournament played there are numerous examples of good thinking that turn likely defeat into success, that nullify the strong points of an opponent; and the 1970 United States Open provided one very striking example in the remarkable success, at the age of thirty-five, of Ken Rosewall.

Ken's main strength is his backhand, and he is known most of all for baseline play, although his net work is particularly smart. On his way to success he defeated some very fine serve-and-net-rushing champions. His smartest thinking was to play throughout the tournament as a net-rusher, even to the degree of taking many risks in returning serve and moving toward the net to about the centre of his court, in the hope that his good return and the added pressure of his speedy movement toward the net would result in an opposition error or a volley opportunity he could turn into a winning point.

There are many enlightening tactical moves in all Rosewall matches, but the one his opponents know best is the way in which he never tries to match the big servers with equal speed. Instead, he concerns himself with accurate placement of his service. If that same opposition is a net-rushing type, then he will quickly find out that the length of Rosewall's serves is going to be as deep as possible; that the percentage of first Rosewall services into court is going to rise even at the expense of a little speed (because Ken knows that most champions automatically move in slightly to receive, and think 'attack' more often when a second service is coming up); and that, after service, Ken will be attacking by moving toward the net faster than usual.

There are countless things to think of on service alone: Occasionally changing your position of service stance in order to confuse your opponent; varying the direction of your service and its pace and style and the direction of your follow-up toward the net—unless, of course, you have found some weakness that is bringing in points; staying back now and again to change a pattern of following first and second services to the net, which, of course, your opponent will know—and especially if you have been caught with short shots to your feet. A change might break the opposition rhythm.

Think. Some of your match thinking should be done before you go on court.

Do you know your opponent's game?

Have you studied it by watching him play matches or even in practice?

Do you recall any helpful points from a previous meeting?

56 Lefthander Neale Fraser, who won Wimbledon in 1960 and the American singles in 1959 and 1960, gives much thought to the preparation of two good-looking steaks when the Davis Cup team rented a flat and did their own household chores. Fraser is best remembered for a big service of pace, swing and kick, a big net game, a strong forehand and a comparatively weak backhand. Because of the disparity in his ground strokes he had to be a 'thinking' player, not only to do what he could with his limited backhand but also to use his best strokes to help protect that weaker side of his game.

56

Do you know his temperament, his fitness, his stamina, his speed about the court, his agility at the net?

If you intend playing tournament tennis you should study your opponent's game; you should keep a record of the players you meet and those you watch, stressing for future use their strengths and weaknesses. Do not trust your memory as to how you fare against some player you may not meet again in a tournament for another year or more.

The usual statistics given on players—about how many backhands they missed, forehands they drove for winners, volleys they netted or smashes they put out—are generally pointless unless you see whether the backhands they played were from difficult positions and whether the forehands were setups; whether the missed volleys were really tough or the smashes that went out were off particularly good lobs. For instance, the missed backhands might have come against a very heavy chop shot, short and angled and with the opponent coming up close to the net. You may not have such an attacking shot in your box of tricks, so when you hit a normal drive to that same backhand it should be handled with ease.

You should watch not only his strokes, but also his attitudes and his habits. For instance, if he is the type who wins a first set and suddenly takes a breather (in other words, decides to take things quietly for a game or two), you must note it carefully so that you can take advantage of it by greater concentration and effort at the appropriate time. Many players do let up at the end of a successful set, even without knowing it. It is partly due to a loss of concentration and partly to the enjoyment of the initial success. Whatever the reason, it is a bad habit. It could provide the opponent with the opportunity of a successful break, which may give him the confidence to improve as the match progresses.

Think. You should be thinking before, during and after each match, each practice session. Perfection in tennis is impossible, which means there is always room for improvement. I used to think, as I travelled the tennis world, that I thought well about the game and thought about it more often than most young players. When I began interesting myself in the development of young players in the hope of making champions of some of them, I began to understand that I had hardly scratched the surface of all there is to know about this wonderful game.

To take one minor example: I found I had believed in my early years that a stroke made on the fast run, to forehand or backhand, was a most difficult stroke to make and a shot seldom successful. I thought a lot about it and came to realize that, as I ran, I could take time to prepare for the stroke because I had distance to cover and I could size up the possibilities of which shot to go for—wide out down-the-line, a top-spin lob or a sharp-angled crosscourt. Because I had time to think, it came to me that the running drive should be a comparatively easy shot to score with. I passed that confidence on to up-and-coming champions, and most of the Davis Cup players of the past twenty-odd years could play it with more than an even chance of scoring. There are countless things to think about. I am sorry I don't have space to talk about more of them.

Practice

Rankings are made on results from match play and never from stories of who beat whom on the practice court.

If you have tennis ambitions you must learn early that the practice court should be used more to iron out weaknesses than practise strengths; that worthwhile practice requires just as much concentration as does good match play; that at times it should be strenuous, because you must often practise as you wish to play matches; and that lack of a companion is no excuse for not practising. If you play a practice match which does not involve selection on some team, you must use it for practice; if you are learning to play net you should go to the net at every opportunity you have—go in and do not worry whether the shot you made is a good one to go in behind. You still get the practice of trying to anticipate where your opponent will play it; if it is played well you still get the experience of trying to reach a tough passing shot or the experience of making a good volley from a difficult position.

If you don't drop-shot well and your practice opponent is reaching what you attempt, don't let that put you off continued drop shot practice. If you are trying to improve the pace and placement of your first or second service, then the practice court is the right place to serve doubles. Don't be upset at practice court losses. At the same time don't turn the game into a complete practice session for yourself to the dissatisfaction of your opponent. You must not be selfish.

Take your practice seriously to the point of concentrating on what you wish to achieve. Try to arrange such games with someone—or several people—you know to be also ambitious and willing to put much effort into their practice. Whenever that type of practice is unavailable, it is certainly worthwhile to take onto the court as many balls as you can muster (the more you have the more time saved) and practise serving for rhythm in your service action, the throw-up of the ball, speed, placement, kick, spin, consistency and so on. The avenues for practice are never-ending. If it helps you to have something to guide you when trying for placement, put an empty box on or near the line you wish to aim for.

The form of practice I have found to be outstanding for general improvement and for sharpening up a champion for a special occasion is called *threes*, often referred to as 'two against one'.

I started this method of practice in the late 1930s in Australia and now it is popular the world over among international players. Its basis is simple and easily understood, and the great need for it is due to the lack of sufficient tournament or match play in which pressure in many forms is such an important factor. Players of all skills can find good stroking form and touch on the practice court, only to find it deserts them in tournament play unless they have been taught to practise under some pressure—the pressure of making accurate passing shots under strong attack. That usually boils down to hitting the ball to the right place at the right speed, and often when moving at top speed, when a point is needed more than usual.

Wherever I have been in the tennis world I have seen more time wasted than put to good use on the practise court, and unfortunately the wasted time is generally among the keen and ambitious youngsters who sometimes wait for hours to get on a court for a short time.

The customary form of practice is for two people, one at each end of the court, to hit the ball to each other as they stand approximately two yards behind the centre of the baseline. They hit down the centre of the court, often taking a short ball on the second or third bounce and seldom moving forward to a very short ball.

This form of practice could be excused if the two players were trying, for five minutes, to accustom themselves to the pace of the court. However, it is just plain stupid if they believe it will make them champions or even improve their games unless they are experimenting with spin, chop, slice, etc.

The ball should not be aimed at the centre of the court except in extreme cases in singles, and in doubles sometimes when there is no understanding between partners about balls 'down the middle', and in doubles again when in doubt what to do with the ball.

In a match one's opponent wants to do anything other than hit the ball back down the centre. His general thought is to hit the ball away from the player the other end of the court. That is the simplest form of strategy. So why practise hitting the ball down the centre? Why stand still and take the ball on second or third bounce when the rules say the ball must be hit on the full or the first bounce?

The basis of *threes* is to provide practice to make winning shots, which usually means using all the court, and often to make those shots under the pressure of running fast after many exchanges in a rally.

As the name suggests, three players are needed on court. The same amount of playing-time should be taken by the 'one' player at one end as by the two against whom he is playing, and valuable time is saved if a large number of balls can be used. Having plenty of balls available also helps to put pressure on the practice from the point of view of physical. fitness.

If I want a player to practise groundstrokes (see diagram I), as if rallying with a singles opponent, he remains backcourt and so do his two opponents, who hit a variety of shots to any part of the singles court. The 'one' player, of course, tries to win the point, but with two opponents in the singles court at the opposite end he finds it difficult. However, it means that he must try all kinds of strokes and use all the court—and if he wishes, he can come to the net on a ball he thinks he can follow-in behind for a winning volley or smash. Even then his smash or volley has to be expertly placed to score against two protecting a singles court.

Next time around, the two at one end could be at the net, as in the accompanying diagram I. From that position they could volley or smash balls within the range the 'one' could cover, including short balls to which he would have to move in fast to reach. The 'one' player should be kept extended, for in that way the pressure is kept on, and it is under this strain that the variety of strokes and shots should be tried.

All three players must, of course, keep well in mind that it is a *practice* court. It is the place where, if you have never before played a top-spin lob, to try it; where you must try the 'outside in' passing shots (the shots made from wide of your own singles line and hit down-the-line to remain wide of the sideline until they pass the net and then land in court near the end of the shot). You must try a short 'dink'—a ball that drops just beyond the net—to the feet of the players at the net, or a very short-angled passing shot, or a fast drive straight at one of the 'two', with racket ready to volley his reply as he defends himself.

The pace of the practice is much faster for the 'one' when two volley at the net, and this means quicker thinking and shorter sessions for each player. It can be hard physically.

Perhaps the toughest form of *threes* is when the 'one' is at the net and kept busy with a mixture of short drives, 'dinks', lobs followed by shots low to the feet as the 'one' tries to get back to the net, and by shots

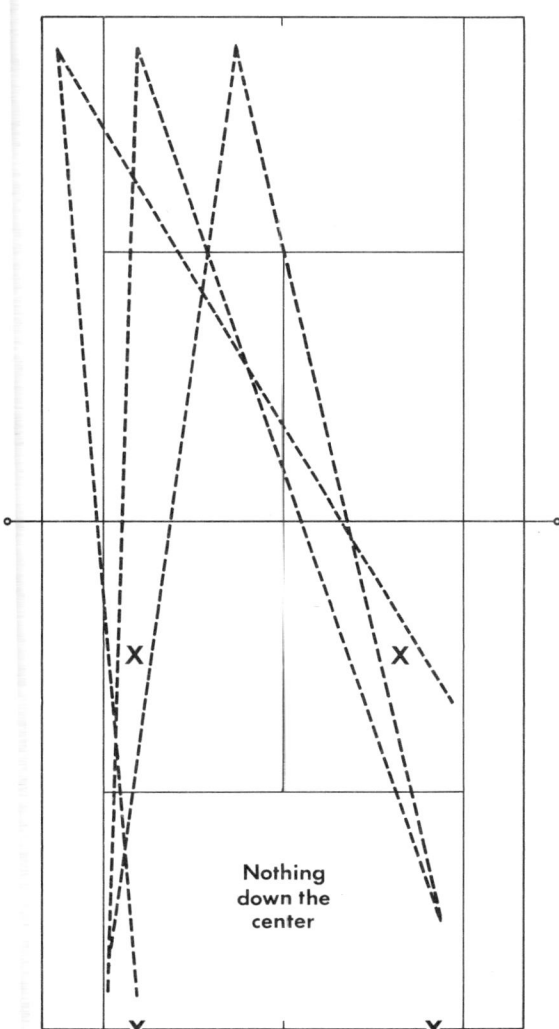

Diagram I I have shown here only the drives from the forehand court. To these can be added chip, chop and slice shots, lobs and all kinds of spin. These same strokes and shots are also tried from the backhand court. This is the part of *threes* practice where two are at the baseline (marked with an X) and 'one' at the other baseline. The same strokes and angles would apply if the two moved in to the net, intercepting drives at about the X marks. This would take the ball back to the 'one' much quicker. The 'one' should mix drives, flat and topped, with other kinds of groundstrokes and 'throw in' plenty of lobs until accuracy can be found with that very important stroke.

Nothing
down the
center

which can just be reached. It is not only wonderful practice, but also a great way to keep match fit.

The idea of most practice is to learn to control the ball to a degree where any stroke can be made with confidence and under pressure in match play, and to make you repeat the shot so often that you will be able to produce it almost automatically at the right time.

As an example of concentration and practice together, I mention one other form of practice among the many I would talk about if space permitted. It is Roy Emerson's service practice. Roy has always believed that he can do better with a medium-paced, consistent and well-placed service—followed by a very fast move toward the net and a good first volley—than with attempts to send down a big delivery all the time. To this end he will serve to the strength of a friend for an hour or more, with the friend trying to beat him with the return while Roy tries not only to reach everything but also to make a first volleying placement with his shot. He is never satisfied simply to put the ball back into play. This is known to top players as a 'gut tearing' way to find form, but Emerson is strong and usually fit and can stand up to it without going stale.

You can understand that he would have to concentrate very closely to follow this form of practice for such a long time. However, when you realize that a match can last for four hours, occasionally longer, you can appreciate that the art of concentration—of giving all your thought to the one match in progress—requires much practice, and so the practice court for any form of play is a very good starting point.

When some champions fall out of form they go to the practice court to (a) watch the ball a little closer onto the racket; (b) pay greater attention to footwork; (c) pay closer attention to backswing or follow-through; (d) concentrate more closely in an effort to 'see' the ball leave the opponent's racket earlier and therefore have more time to reach the ball; (e) practise the service if it was giving trouble, or do a hundred and one things on court which could help; and then (f), perhaps, go for a run with some short, sharp sprints.

I tell what the champion will sometimes do with the thought that this book could be of value to players of all ages and categories. You may not be out of form, but there is almost certainly some room for improvement in your game. By reading this you may be able to analyse your own strokes, tactics and temperament in relation to some basic principles of the game; decide to experiment with some of the 'racket work' shots you see the champions bring off; or even change your lack of midweek preparation for a weekend to a preparation which takes little time but does you a lot of good physically, and also improves your confidence and your tennis repute. Try it. You might find what I have discovered from experience of over fifty years' playing: one is never too old to learn.

Wall practice

Practice does not always make perfect but there is no doubt that it has produced many very good tennis players. No tennis club for juniors should be without a wall against which to practise; this provides the opportunity for the slightly more ambitious youngster to practise just that little bit more—and this so often makes all the difference in a match.

No one with a wall and 10 to 15 yards of space in front of it can be excused for not practising tennis. Ideally the surface in front of the wall should be even, to make groundstrokes bound truly; preferably, but not necessarily, the wall should exceed 6 feet in width and 6 feet in height— with netting above it; this will provide worthwhile practice.

The wall can be brick, wood (a garage door, perhaps, with a couple of stays at the back to strengthen it), large wooden double gates, the sides of two or three large packing cases or even something like strong netting held taut between posts.

If the surface in front of the wall is level, ground strokes should be practised with the aims of: watching the ball right onto the racket; improving footwork by hitting so that forehands and backhands are played alternately and so that a ball occasionally comes back straight at you (footwork must therefore be sharp); hitting some shots to the height of the net (which you could mark on the hitting surface) and some to 2 feet above that mark; change of pace; and a change of drives to chops and slices, drop shots and the different spins.

The wider the practice wall the better, of course, because it will give you the opportunity to practise strokes played on the run as you angle your shot to the wall and will enable you to send back different angles. You can't beat the wall, so mistakes are unimportant. Don't practise only the shots you like best.

SERVICE

You can practise service whether or not you have a half-court—baseline to the net—distance. If you have about half the usual distance, aim about 12 to 18 inches above the net line marked on the board, and when you wish to practise a swing service—if, for instance, you want to swing a service wide to an opponent in the forehand (first) court—stand wide and not necessarily in front of the wall, as if you were standing a few yards from the centre of the baseline.

A wall is ideal for practising the throw-up of the ball—for the correct consistency in the height you wish to contact the ball, and also for the accurate position in front of and above your head—or some other position depending on the type of service you wish to practise.

SMASH

In most cases a good server smashes well, but never take it for granted that serving practice alone will take care of your smashing. The racket action of the smash is usually similar to a flat or slightly sliced service. There is a lot of difference, however, in the two strokes: one of them finds the player stationary and hitting a ball that is barely moving; while in going for an overhead (or smash) the player usually has to move, often fast and sometimes with a jump, and maintain balance, for the ball is moving rapidly. Stand about 2 or 3 yards from the wall; hit the ball to the ground about 2 to 3 feet in front of the wall so that it hits the wall as it rises and continues up over your head (see diagram J). Trial and error will show you the right distance at which to make the ball come off the wall in such a way that you must move back sharply as the ball goes over your head. The smash must be aimed down in front of the wall to about the same spot so as to bring the ball back for another smash. This can be repeated endlessly, depending on your accuracy in smashing to the right spot and on your fitness. You can vary the smash's height and distance back from the wall by the pace with which you hit and by the distance from which you smash each shot.

It is not easy at first to smash in such a way that you will bring the ball back as another smash, but that will come with practice. Meanwhile, it is excellent practice to try to play whatever your smash does bring back. When you do find control, don't stand in the one spot; it is better practice to move forward to a short shot which may even be a high volley and then move back for a deep smash.

Playing against the wall is a good way to practise your movement backward to take a high lob. Avoid a number of small shuffling steps as you begin to move backward, and try to learn to get off the mark with a couple of fast, long steps.

Many people smash their best when they jump off the ground, even if it is only a few inches. Try it that way; try it any way until you find which is best for you—you can afford to do so because one of the fine things about a wall is that *it* never tires!

Smashing can be gut-tearing, but it is good for you and usually fun because there is nothing more satisfying in the game than to make a smashing winner with power and placement from a deep lob. There have been many who could do just that, and there are some great overhead players today who seldom miss a smash from any part of the court. I mention Ken Rosewall's smashing as he won the United States Open of 1970 because he did not miss one smash and won most of them outright—and he is approximately 5 feet 7 inches tall. In other words, a player does not have to be tall to smash well. There have been many small and agile players with as good an overhead as any tall player.

Don't neglect the backhand smash—and the wall is the best place to practise it. It is excellent practice to alternate with a ball to your right side and then one to your left for smashing. The backhand smash usually feels very clumsy, but practice will smooth out the awkward action very quickly.

VOLLEYING

Stand 4 to 5 yards from the wall with as many balls as you can hold. Hit the ball to the wall hard enough to take the return on the volley either forehand or backhand—or anyhow. I mean anyhow. Don't let a ball get past you, if possible, for you will be practising in order to quicken your reflexes as well as to improve the stroking of the forehand and backhand volleys.

Don't necessarily stand still. Move about as you reach for balls which don't come off the wall as you anticipated.

As you learn to handle the pace at which you start to rally with your volleys, increase the pace slowly. I am sure you will be pleasantly surprised at how much you will improve with constant practice and at how fast you begin to move your racket to meet balls that you would not previously have even tried to play.

There is additional fun in this wall practice by playing those balls which are hit between your feet or on your left side and close to your body, i.e. those balls you cannot get your racket to in the usual way.

These shots are usually played 'blindly', with the racket swung behind the body between the feet, or just to the left side, without thought of how the racket will be facing. It is just as easy—with practice—to swing your racket into position for such shots so that the full face of the racket is in the direction from which the ball is coming.

Practise it; it is quite a thrill to connect properly with such shots, and not nearly as difficult as it may seem when you watch the champions doing it.

LOW VOLLEYING

Now stand further back from the wall, perhaps another yard or two, and, hitting the ball at about the same pace as for the volley, take the ball closer to the ground for the low volley. Like all the other strokes of the game this requires much practice, and you can get, in half an hour on the wall, more low volleys than you would get in two hundred sets of play. Such low volleys are short blocking strokes in the main, both on the forehand and the backhand, and you must get down to the ball well balanced so as to have complete command of your racket, for the face of the racket does most of the directing of the ball.

RUNNING BACK TO LOB

You cannot practise the lob (sometimes called the toss) against the wall, but you can practise running back to lob. By smashing the ball down in front of the wall with more power than when looking for a smash, you will get something like a deep lob. Learn to run for the ball not directly under it, but slightly to the right—if you are a righthander. In this way you will be in position to play it on the bound without having to side-shuffle or skip around it, as so many do when they run back for a lob directly under the flight of the ball.

Diagram J Wall practice lob

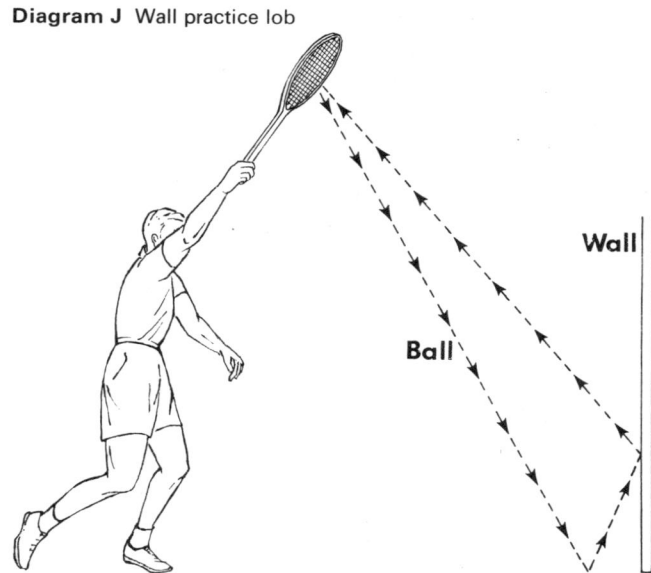

84

Shadow stroking

For many years I have used a form of practice that I call 'shadow stroking' to aid my own game and to try to help others. I recommend it to be used in good or poor weather, inside or outside. It can be used singly or for a class, but for class coaching the group should be kept small so that the instructor can keep a check on the stroking of each pupil.

I use it to check my own stroking, for footwork especially, and for fitness. In this form of practice I watch: (a) the bending low for the imaginary low ball and getting up high with body, arm and stroke for the high bounce; (b) good, fast footwork moving out to the imaginary wide ball with good balance at the end of the stroke so that recovery can be quick; (c) movement of the racket (a must) so that it is well behind the ball just before impact, thus preventing a rushed swing at the last moment; (d) the good, firm control of the follow-through, with the racket head finishing at a suitable angle, had you wanted to try varying the stroke; and (e) the fast, smooth sideways skip back to the original position while watching the imaginary ball you stroked.

In the case of the backhand most players should watch carefully for the most common fault found with strokes on this side, which is not turning the body far enough sideways to allow for a long backswing. I suggest you take another look at the backhand chapter before making that stroke in shadow stroking.

You can shadow practise on your own, but it is more fun and better for you if you have someone out in front calling the stroke. It makes you more inclined to be quickly off the mark—it is most important to react rapidly. Make sure you move a few steps towards the imaginary ball most of the time—not always, because some of the imaginary strokes will be for the ball coming straight towards you. In this case you must sidestep to play forehand or backhand, whichever you prefer for the shot you are about to make. Don't simply turn and stroke; use your feet, for in doing so not only will you get practice for strokes that you will most often play in matches, but you will also get more exercise and that should lead to greater fitness.

If you have doubts that this can be good exercise, try the low volley and smash practice. At the call of 'low volley' you should move forward several paces half-crouched, prepared for a very low ball, and make a firm block volley (not a swing, please). Having given you time to make that imaginary volley the caller will say 'smash'. You must move back fast, with even paces if possible, and get up into the air for the imaginary lob. As you land you will hear 'low-backhand volley' and you move forward—again half-crouched and with speed—to block a volley before moving back and up again for another smash.

This needs practice to be done smoothly, and you must be alert for the trap of too much foot shuffling with little steps as the backward movement for the smash begins. Remember: one good step to start.

Repeat this volley-smash exercise (concentrating on low volleys on the forehand and backhand sides) a dozen times, and I am sure you will agree that it is good for training.

You can go through your whole repertoire of strokes in this fashion, changing from stroke to stroke rapidly at times to help keep reflexes sharp. If indoors, and a mirror is in a handy position, take the opportunity of looking at your strokes, studying them for backswing, the beginning of spin, flat, chop or slice control, point of contact and follow-through and, of course, footwork and weight distribution.

Don't rush this shadow stroking. Make sure you are alert to the various strokes with the speed necessary in match play, but don't let them become sloppy; finish each stroke correctly before moving back to your original position.

Very important: Don't neglect to watch that imaginary ball—in the same way that you should watch the real ball on court—right onto your racket.

As a footnote to the above I recall that one time I was telling a group of youngsters they could practise shadow stroking indoors if it was too wet outside. A mother who was listening said, 'Mr Hopman, what happens to my furniture, to the lights?' My answer was that an old broken racket could be found and the handle, a little longer than the grip, cut off. Perhaps you can make that grip 'racket-heavy' with lead or something similar. If you cannot find an old racket to cut down, then use part of a broom handle.

'Scramble'

'Yet honour he,
Who wounded sore
Sinks foiled
But fighting evermore.'

In practice with youngsters who are keen, I call loudly to them to pick up their racket if they drop it and then hit a ball near them giving them a chance to recover to make a stroke and return the ball.

I have no time for the gifted youngster who feels it below his status to scramble in this way. Give me the player who will chase everything, and if he has only one leg, I feel I can make something of him.

I am proud of the evident fact that every Australian champion who played in the Davis Cup during the past twenty years scrambled. I taught them to 'run down' almost anything in practice and they did it in matches. Frank Sedgman was the first of them, and there are tennis enthusiasts I meet these days who recall his great speed around the court and his many miraculous 'gets'. As it happened, I asked Frank to come to a coaching class I used to conduct after school on Thursday afternoons at Kooyong (Melbourne and Victorian tennis headquarters), because I liked his smile and the way he chased everything. That was 1939 when he was twelve years old.

Enthusiasts who talk now of Ken McGregor, Lew Hoad, Ken Rosewall, Neale Fraser, Rod Laver, Roy Emerson and others never fail to mention their ability to scramble, to return the 'impossible', to stretch to their utmost to prevent a ball passing them and to leap up and up to bring one down.

Many a player who has opposed Emerson knows he has made mistakes —many more than usual—trying to hit the ball closer and closer to the lines, trying to put it out of 'Emmo's' reach.

America's top champion of the early 1960s, Chuck McKinley, was renowned for his great retrieving ability and his willingness to 'throw himself' at the ball in his effort to get it back.

Cliff Richey is the current great scrambler among America's top players and he retrieves many shots which appear to be winners.

87

57 A young scrambler, Jaime Krombluh, Scarsdale, New York, aged nine

57

You learn to scramble in practice. A youngster I reprimanded for not going 'all the way' after a shot told me he had let it go so he could get back quickly to play the next shot from inside the court. Because he had played little match tennis I found it difficult to convince him that a great 'get' which eventually leads to winning a point is worth much more than a glorious drive to an empty corner. Such a 'get' will earn respect as a fighter, a 'battler', from opponents, and such repute is worth many points.

88

Physical fitness

A tennis player with ambition should practise moderation in everyday habits, with full knowledge that over-indulgence in any phase of living is generally a handicap on the court and often leads to the loss of an essential prized by most who wish to play sport well—sleep.

I always sought to organize Australia's Davis Cup players into normal lives, at the same time fitting many hours of practice, training or match play into most days. With some of the top team players in their 'teens, sleep meant rest for building bodies as well as recovering from tiring tennis days. There was never any set hour for all members of a team to retire.

The young players in all teams drank a good deal of milk and the older players were sometimes allowed to drink beer if they had earned it by plenty of training or match play, and generally speaking the older players were those in their middle or late twenties. Few of the Australian Davis Cup players smoked, and two of this small number, Roy Emerson and Fred Stolle, smoked a token few because of their goodwill association with cigarette manufacturing companies. I used to watch the beer drinkers carefully because of the difficulty many young people have in telling an obliging hostess, or others doing the rounds with a jug, that beer was beer regardless of who poured it into a glass.

The main accent in training for tennis should be on strengthening the legs, arms, lungs, wrists and the stomach muscles and on sharpening up the reflexes. Running is excellent for the legs and lungs, with distances for stamina and sharp bursts of short sprints to keep a player conditioned for the many bursts of speed necessary in getting to the net, moving across it, back to the back court for lobs and for the many points a good player must scramble for in top company.

Double knee jumps (with the knees rising to touch the chest) and push-ups are good for the legs, chest and stomach muscles, and, of course, push-ups are also good for the wrists and arms. Sit-ups, too, are excellent for the stomach muscles.

Slow high-knee running, lifting the knees as high as possible, is good for the legs and general fitness.

I like the double knee jumps also for agility; other exercises for the same purpose include jumping into a jackknife, kangaroo hops and any twisting and jumping. All forms of skipping are excellent for legs, agility and general

58

fitness. There are many more simple exercises which can be done without apparatus and, of course, still more if one can work in a gymnasium.

In the early days of their careers some of the Australian Davis Cup players did some weightlifting to put on muscle, but none used it as a means to keep fit once they reached championship classes. Occasionally they would have a little fun with weightlifting bets.

I have such a false reputation for being a slave driver of young and ambitious tennis players that it may sound strange that I advise you to be very careful not to overtrain for a tournament. If a player anticipates doing well in one or more events of a tournament, he should go into it fit but certainly not trained down to the 'last pound he can lose' like a boxer 'making weight'. A tournament during the summer and running through a week with the finalists playing one, two and sometimes three matches each day (if in singles, doubles and mixed doubles or in junior and senior events) can be exhausting, and a player sometimes needs to lose a little surplus so as to be ready—but not overdone—for the finals.

It is not necessary for someone already in good shape to sweat profusely when running. In summer training I advise light clothes unless you aim to lose weight. And there is no reason to run miles and miles without a stop.

59 Rod Laver, Neale Fraser and Roy Emerson in the front row, all Wimbledon and American championship winners, demonstrate the double-knee jump with knees up to the chest and the jump high. Extreme left is Bob Mark, who was of the same Davis Cup 'hope' vintage as Laver but left Australia to try his tennis fortunes in South Africa. I'm calling the exercises at bottom right and the best I can say for the other two visible in the picture, Mike Sangster in the centre, and Wayne Reid, is that they 'missed the jump'.

60 Phil Dent was 'out of step' with Tony Roche, Bill Bowrey and Ray Ruffels in this little workout, but it serves my purpose well. The kangaroo hop starts with 'Dentie' and goes up with Tony, Bill and Ray, comes back to 'Dentie's' squat and up we go again — and again — and again.

60

Often it is better for your tennis for you to concentrate on sprints which comprise jogging 20 to 30 yards and sprinting about the same distance and repeating this two or three times in the same run. Stop until breathing is normal and then repeat until you think you have done enough for the day. Be careful not to pull up sharply at the end of each sprint. Carelessness in this respect could cost a pulled muscle.

Illustration 59 here is easy to follow for the double knee jump. Push-ups are simply pushing your body weight up from a flat position on the floor with your hands palms-down under your chest, while keeping the body stiff. Sit-ups are lying on your back and raising your head and back up and forward so that your head touches — or goes close to — your ankles, which should be kept together. If it helps, the feet can be placed under something like the framework of a bed or a heavy chair.

High-knee running explains itself; lift the knees higher than usual and 'run on the spot'.

In the kangaroo hop (see picture 60) you begin standing and sink to a squatting position. Then leap upward as high as possible with hands outstretched above your head, only to come down again, on your toes, and repeat the leap upward. Warm up before you do this one because it can be tough on the muscles at the back of the legs.

If you are unaccustomed to these exercises and wish to do them, I suggest you begin with only a few of each and later, as you get to know them, increase the number of times for each.

92

Running in the rain

If you are ambitious to improve your tennis, don't sit around on a wet day doing nothing if indoor tennis is unavailable. You can shadow stroke; you can work in the gymnasium; you can read tennis or talk to someone with experience to back their words; and you can go running in the rain. I am sure Frank Sedgman, Ken McGregor, Merv Rose, Ken Rosewall, Lew Hoad, Mal Anderson, Ashley Cooper, Neale Fraser, Rod Laver, Fred Stolle, John Newcombe and Tony Roche know more parks, gardens, school fields or golf courses on which they can run as they tour around the world than all the top players of the world over the past twenty years of any other five countries put together. I guarantee they would know those running tracks when wet far better than other tennis players.

Our teams, touring for six to eight months of each year, seldom wasted a day when rain washed out play. They would probably go to the cinema, but only after a run in the rain. Old, light clothes, no shoes and sometimes a plastic head cover if worried about a cold would be the order of the day; this also included getting out of their wet things immediately they returned to their hotel.

Try it sometime: A run in the rain is a tonic, especially when followed by a shower and brisk rubdown.

Match preparation

Reasons (or excuses if you wish) for tournament matches lost by all standards of players, from novice to champion, include carelessness and lack of experience in preparation.

The most important approach to a match is to be as normal as possible. True, the match is more important than an average game, and for that very reason most players do find themselves 'on their toes' in spirit, if not literally, but they should approach a match in much the same way as a normal game. For instance, many players have lost tomorrow's match by retiring too early—much earlier than usual and without some exceptional reason for tiredness. They have not been sleepy and, while waiting for sleep, have begun thinking of the match and have remained in that state for too long.

How much sleep should one get before a match? That is as individual a matter as eating or drinking and must sometimes be qualified by the time of play. Some tournaments begin early in the morning, and if a player is drawn for an early match, the time of the first morning meal—and how much to eat—have to be considered.

Some people digest food more easily than others. Keep it well in mind that a match will not be played only on the energy from that day's food but also on fitness, strength and stamina built up over a period of time. If you are running late for a match and you believe a morning meal is imperative before a morning match, then have the meal but cut down on quantity. Be careful: don't eat everything simply because it is placed on your plate.

You must get to know yourself in respect of what you prefer to eat at certain hours before play and how much is best for you. Don't allow a stranger, trying to be kind, to say what is best for you.

If your match is delayed and you feel hungry, then eat a small amount of something you believe is beneficial.

If the type of food you like before tennis is not available at the tournament, make sure you take along what you want the next day.

If you think you may worry too much or you believe watching tennis may tire you, take along something to read.

If the weather is cold take the right kind of clothes in which to sit around; and make sure you are warm when you step onto court. Keep in touch with the tournament manager: ask for advance warning before you have to play so as to warm up by jogging, calisthenics or hitting a ball about if there is a practice court or wall.

Your preparation should not finish there. If the weather is hot you may need a tennis hat, salt tablets, sweat bands and something to drink (perhaps something special if you don't like the water or soft drink supplied).

Don't be careless; don't take risks. Try to look at this preparation in the light of all your time, training and practice in order to help you reach the level of acceptance into the tournament.

Selection of equipment

Imagine spending months preparing for a tournament, the excitement of reaching the final, and then, on an important point at a critical stage of that final, a string in your favourite racket breaks.

It does happen. I have watched it happen and later listened to the 'if only' lament.

Often such laments are unnecessary. Care of your equipment is vital, as is the inspection of your rackets before match play.

The selection of a tennis racket is almost as personal as the choice of an evening gown or one's taste in food. A frail-looking girl may have a very strong wrist but she would probably do best with a light racket because she wants to play a net-attacking game. The slight man with the comparatively weak wrist might do better with a heavier racket because he does not wish to run much and believes he wants a heavy racket to make the most of what strokes he does get the chance to make. The person best suited to select a racket for you, if you are inexperienced, is the experienced friend who plays, the coach at the club or the experienced sporting goods salesman.

There is no limit to the size or weight of rackets, but the average for men is $13\frac{3}{4}$ ounces and $13\frac{1}{2}$ for women. Rackets vary according to one's build and power. A well-grown girl should be able to use a 13, and a well-built boy a 13 to $13\frac{1}{2}$. Trial and error is the best way to find the right one, and at most tennis centres and clubs it is customary for a player to borrow a racket for a few games to try out a different weight or balance, if concerned about the racket he, or she, is using.

The grip is just as personal as the racket weight and balance. The average grip is $4\frac{1}{2}$ to $4\frac{5}{8}$ inches in circumference, both for men and women. Some prefer much smaller or much larger grips and this preference is not always related to the length of the fingers or the size of the hand. There is even a difference of opinion over whether a large or small grip gives more wrist freedom. I myself believe the smaller grip allows greater freedom.

The normal racket is 27 inches long, and so the balance point for an evenly balanced racket should be $13\frac{1}{2}$ inches from either end. Most sports shops will sell a rubber band which can be stretched around the centre of the face of the head of the frame to make up for the weight of the strings to be used. I believe it is impossible to know for certain whether an evenly-balanced, a light-headed or a handle-heavy racket is best for any player without seeing him play. However, in general someone with less than average wrist strength should avoid a heavy-headed racket.

Most, but not all, of the champions have their rackets strung tightly, but it would be a mistake to suggest all players should follow this custom. On the contrary, I believe that the majority of players have their rackets too tight, considering the lack of opportunities to practise and the fact that, generally speaking, the tighter the racket the better the timing must be. Most rackets are strung to certain poundages with 65 to 68 being regarded as tight. However, I have found that most stringers have their own methods of ascertaining poundage—even in an age of stringing-machines—and therefore the poundage system for stringing is unreliable.

When not in use rackets should be kept away from changing atmospheric conditions. Don't leave them in a closet where, for instance, skiing equipment will be stored during the winter or raincoats hung. A cover and a press are additional protection, provided the press is put on the racket correctly, with even pressure on the frame.

Just as much care should be taken in the selection of shoes as of rackets, because impaired footwork is a greater handicap than a broken string or a slightly warped racket. Also your tennis clothing should be comfortable, especially if you wear a sun hat. If you do, and if the weather is very hot and your head gets hot under the hat, don't keep the headgear on all the time. Take it off, perhaps, at times when the sun is not bothering you, and definitely take it off while changing ends in order to allow some air to get at your head.